Esther's Gospel

The God Who Is There

Tim Merwin

Thank you for purchasing this book!

Connect with Tim:

Subscribe to **Gospel Connections** blog at:

www.timmerwin.com

Or, if you prefer, connect with Tim on:

"I am so glad Tim preached through the book of Esther in his local church, and I am even more thrilled that he has written this book about it! Because Tim is a good friend, I've had the benefit of reading **Esther's Gospel** as if I'm in that coffee shop with Tim listening to him tell the story of Esther. The Tim that I know is the same Tim I've encountered on the pages of this book. I don't know about you, but I like that. It lends credibility to the material.

The book of Esther is "in" Tim so that for our benefit it could come "out of" Tim. What comes out is a faithful, encouraging, inspiring, sometimes humorous, and always Christ-exalting understanding of why the book of Esther is preserved in Holy Scripture. Tim will help you to see how one book of the Bible is seamlessly woven into the storyline of Scripture; the story of God's plan through Jesus to redeem sinful man. You will discover new insights on Esther, and yet find it very familiar to the Old Story. God bless your reading of this book. I hope you'll take the time with the reflection questions over a cup of coffee, and find your heart stirred by grace as I have mine!"

> **Aron Osborne** Pastor, Metro Life Church and Director, Grace Partnership

"Tim Merwin's new book, **Esther's Gospel, The God who IS there**, is faith-building, challenging, and filled with wisdom for every believer. By setting the context with interesting historical background, Tim not only helps the readers better understand the passage but gives them a feel for what it would have been like to be there. And behind all the history, worldly kingdoms, decisions, plots, schemes and failures of the book's characters, there is a King who is sovereign over all, who causes all things to work for his glory and the good of his people. Tim compassionately identifies with those who struggle, suffer and wonder where God is in their pain, by sharing some of his own struggles with cancer and Crohn's disease. And most importantly, Tim shows us how the book of Esther, which makes no mention of God, clearly displays the glory of Jesus Christ and the gospel. This book will be a blessing to Christians but also one that can be shared with non-Christian friends as well."

> **Mark Altrogge** Pastor, songwriter, and writer at theblazingcenter.com

"Is Esther more than a pretty face? Tim Merwin looks beneath the familiar outlines to show how Christ is woven throughout her story. Tim's pastoral heart, humor, and commitment to God's glory shine through his writing. Take a look through his eyes. You'll see Esther for who she really is."

Linda Evans, Founder, Pregnancy Resources Melbourne http://melbournepri.com

"Behold our God! I have known Tim and his family for many years and he has stood amazed at the glory of God. Tim shows us God and all His glory through unpacking Esther. This book will refresh you with God's grace for the undeserving and will inspire you to trust Him even when you don't see Him in life's circumstances. Throughout this book and when you have finished, surely you will say, "Behold our God! Enjoy!"

Phil Courson, Senior Pastor, Abundant Grace Community Church

"I have long loved the story of Esther. But not like this. Tim sheds much light on the account by sharing much of the historical backdrop. When you see the driving motivations of the players in light of their history, it becomes much easier to see the God of the Bible, at work through these ordinary people. Mistakes made, lives at risk, all the drama you could ever want in a novel, and yet, it's right here on the pages of Scripture. Read this book, and find your own story of God's glory."

John Morgan, Author of *War On Fear* and George W. Bush Renowned Impressionist: www.johncmorgan.com

To my amazing wife, Kim.

As we have walked, laughed, and cried together, we have found the glory of Christ's gospel on every page of our lives. I look forward to writing the next chapters of life with you. Thanks for saying "I do"

I love you!

Foreword By Daniel Henderson

Preface: A Word About God's Word

Acknowledgments

Introduction: God, Gospel, And Esther

Foreword By Daniel Henderson

Tim Merwin has delivered an unexpected treasure from an underestimated text in *Esther's Gospel*. Since I first met Tim several years ago I have admired his passion for Jesus, enduring faith and incredible love for the church. Having read *Esther's Gospel*, I am astounded by his clarity and, frankly, his courage in unpacking such relevant truth from the often-dismissed book of Esther – a book that even Martin Luther thought was "quite underwhelming." No more.

As Tim has admitted, "Some assign the book of Esther to stay within the walls of the children's ministry. Others view it as nothing more than a good moral story, for such a time as this. And, to others, Esther has all the pieces to be little more than a cute Christianized Cinderella romance novel. After all, there's the powerful and wealthy king, a royal palace complete with lavish banquets, and, we must not forget, the beautiful maiden in distress. Furthermore, our little story includes the drama of divorce and the pursuit of a new, young and beautiful wife."

But as you will soon discover, the story of Esther has compelling relevance to our lives. Some have wondered, "Where is God in the story of Esther?" As Tim points out so practically, many of us are asking right now, "Where is God in the story of my life?" This book provides a riveting and solidly-biblical application of God's truth and presence in your comfort, in your suffering, in your uncertainties and in your questions about the out-of-control world in which we live.

The greatest spiritual failure in any life is to reject the gospel of Christ. One of the most tragic spiritual mistakes for a Christian is the neglect of a gospel mindset in all of life. Without this mindset, a believer fails to see and savor the glory of the gospel in the entirety of the Bible. While many would place Esther at the bottom of the list of gospel-oriented books, Tim masterfully and meaningfully elevates the profound and practical value of this inspired story. He also provides us with new eyes to see the gospel with fresh gratitude.

John Piper has written, "The ultimate aim of the gospel is the display of God's glory and the removal of every obstacle to our seeing it and savoring it as our highest treasure. "Behold Your God!" is the most gracious command and the best gift of the gospel. If we do not see Him and savor Him as our greatest fortune, we have not obeyed or believed the gospel." [1]

I believe as you read *Esther's Gospel* you will truly "Behold Your God!" Old obstacles will be removed and a new savoring will emerge in your soul. As he concludes, Tim offers us the hope and challenge that we will treasure Christ, grow in Christ and proclaim Christ. As we embrace this we have rediscovered the core essence of God's plan for us on this earth. We will have fresh faith to recognize God in our story. And we will find ourselves re engaging with God in HIS story. Be assured, it is a profound and purposeful story. A story we are privileged to experience and exhibit for Christ's glory.

Daniel Henderson

Founder and President–Strategic Renewal International (strategicrenewal.com)

Author of *Transforming Prayer* and *Old Paths, New Power*

---

[1] John Piper, God Is the Gospel: Meditations on God's Love as the Gift of Himself (Wheaton, Ill: Crossway, 2011) 56

Preface: **A Word About God's Word**

Blessed is the man who walks

not in the counsel of the wicked,

nor stands in the way of sinners,

Nor sits in the seat of scoffers;

but his delight is in the law of the LORD,

and on his law he meditates day and night.

He is like a tree

planted by streams of water

that yields its fruit in its season,

and its leaf does not wither.

In all that he does, he prospers.

The wicked are not so,

but are like chaff that the wind drives away.

Therefore the wicked will not stand in the judgment,

nor sinners in the congregation of the righteous;

for the LORD knows the way of the righteous,

but the way of the wicked will perish.

Psalm 1

Glory is to be mined and discovered within the pages God's Word. Its wisdom is yet to be exhausted, its beauty never fully beheld. The Word contains glories for created man to stand before and behold in awesome wonder. These infinite glories reveal that God's perfect plan, Christ's redemption, and the Spirit's work are nothing less than mind-boggling, dazzling aspects of His amazing grace!

Psalm one launches the Psalter by presenting us with two roads. One is the road of blessedness (Happiness and Joy) found in the wisdom and counsel of God's Word. The other is the road of the wicked. Unfortunately, it's not hard to admit that I have too often not delighted in His Word and instead sought the well-traveled road of wickedness. With Psalm 1 in mind, my prayer for myself and you, the reader, is that this book might, in small or large ways, draw you to that blessed road. That happy road is found by planting oneself by those streams of water, the very words of God. I pray you might know the fruits that are yielded by those water streams. Let us together renounce this world's foolish counsel, forsake its wisdom, and reject the road that leads to death. And let us behold the glory of our God as we delight and meditate on Him.

Soli Deo Gloria

Acknowledgments

Thank you to the church I call home, Trinity Community Church, whose pursuit of the Lord has greatly shaped the way I think about Esther and the Gospel. I thank God for the privilege of serving and worshiping our God together as we live out our days for the glory of our King! Every day of the last 21+ years that we have walked together has been a journey blessed by God. I love you, church!

To the elders I have been given the benefit of serving with: (Mace, Rick, Nate, and Alex) thanks for your care and friendship. I join with Paul in saying, *"I thank my God in all my remembrance of you....because of your partnership in the gospel..."*

To my family: (Tanner, Timothy, Tyler and Maddie, Kaylee and Sidney, and my wife Kim): I am a husband and father blessed beyond measure because of each of you! I love you and thank God for you!

To my Savior, Jesus Christ: Thank you for your life, death, and resurrection. I remain forever grateful!

Introduction: God, Gospel, And Esther

Across the table sat my friend; we relaxed at the cafe´ enjoying coffee, chatting about God's Word, and generally catching up on life. I had been studying and preparing for a "Coming Soon" series to preach at the church that I call home, Trinity Community Church. The conversation and the coffee were both brewed rich and bold. Genuinely interested, my friend asked: "What are you preaching at Trinity?" "Esther," I replied. And then "it" happened. And, "it" would happen many more times over the course of the next year.

What do I mean by "it" happened? Well, "it" is a certain look. "It" is a sideways glance or an expression that communicates: *Esther? Why Esther? The Bible is a big book with so much to glean from, why Esther? Why not preach on something more relevant or interesting? After all, what does Esther have to do with my life today?*

This coffee conversation became a common occurrence with men and women, pastors and members, friends and acquaintances. I began to second-guess myself. *Am I crazy or does this little book have more to offer than the regularly repeated phrase from Esther: "for such a time as this"?*[1] As I sought to write this book, many asked: "What are you writing?" And, "it" continued to happen.

I'm okay with the inquiry. Certainly, it's not the first time that someone had questions about this little book that's tucked away in the Bible's Old Testament. "Why Esther?" is not a crazy question. After all, the Old Testament is, well, old. Worse yet, the book of Esther never mentions God, not even once! What are we to think of a book in the Bible that doesn't mention God?

---

[1] If you are not familiar with the phrase, "for such a time as this…." it comes from Esther 4:14. Esther is being challenged by Mordecai to risk her life "for such a times as this…" to save her fellow Jews.

The New Testament seems to be in agreement in thinking little of the book. Jesus and the apostles never so much as give a tip of the hat to Esther, never quoting or alluding to the book. Perhaps these are reasons why Martin Luther thought that the book of Esther was quite underwhelming, concluding that it should not have been included in the canon.[2] He said, "I am so great an enemy to... Esther, that I wish [it] had not come to us at all, for [it has] too many heathen unnaturalities."[3] One commentary had these unflattering thoughts towards Esther: "It's a very good book, but I don't recommend preaching Esther."[4] I can't help but wonder what your perspective might be of this little book nestled in the pages of the Old Testament.

Some assign the book of Esther to stay within the walls of children's ministry. Others view it as nothing more than a good moral story, "for such a time as this...." where we are inspired to live courageously like Esther. To others, Esther has all the pieces to be little more than a cute, Christianized Cinderella romance novel. After all, there's the powerful and wealthy king, a royal palace complete with lavish banquets, and we must not forget the beautiful maiden in distress. Furthermore, our little story includes the drama of divorce and the pursuit of a new, young and beautiful wife.

Yes, the book of Esther has all the makings of a Hollywood summer blockbuster. I am not a big fan of Hollywood's interpretations of God's Word. Recently, I had a free evening and, in a moment of desired mindlessness, I decided to check out Hollywood's perspective on Esther. I grabbed the first Esther movie that popped up on my Netflix feed and, against my better judgment, began to watch. Now, you need to know that I am a merciless movie critic. I don't like most movies. I am sure I am not the only one who is tired of worn out oversimplified plots, bad acting, and explosive scenes that are supposed to wow me...but don't.

---

[2] Note: There is much debate on Luther's view of Esther. I am not dogmatic on my opinion, but it does seem likely Luther was not an enthusiastic supporter of the book of Esther.

[3] Luther, Martin, "Of God's Word: XXIV" [1566], in *The Table-Talk of Martin Luther*, trans. William Hazlitt, Philadelphia: Lutheran Publication Society, 1893.

[4] I read this in a commentary too many years ago to remember where I read it and thus this quote is not cited.

I anticipated that this was going to be a bad movie night but nothing had prepared me for what I was about to see. I watched as the king's chariot rode through the village, casting dust upon a common woman. Wealth and royalty intersected with the poverty of a commoner. In a magical moment, the two unlikely lovers caught each other's eyes. Sparks flew. It was quick, very quick, but the viewer instantly knew that the genre of the movie would be an unlikely romance. As I watched the scene unfold, I tried to imagine the production team gathered around the large conference table, discussing how they were going to weave the classic Cinderella story into *Esther: the Movie.*

I realized I was supposed to watch this movie with excited anticipation: *how will this budding romance unfold?* That is the point of the book of Esther. Isn't it? I endured and pushed forward until I came to the scene of the king and Esther in his bed chamber. The virtuous king desires to have her but (cue the music) he will wait for the wedding night. "Are you kidding me?" I groaned at my TV. "Is this why Esther takes up valuable space in the Bible?" If I continued to watch, I might have found myself to be in agreement with Luther! I was unable to muster the strength required to finish the movie. Knowing how I would feel ninety minutes later, I determined to end my misery. I haven't watched another Esther movie since. I know. I know. I never found out if the virtuous, wealthy king and poverty struck, Cinderella - Esther married. I will never know if they lived happily ever after riding off into the sunset on the king's horse drawn chariot.

Hollywood aside, how do you tell the story of Esther? It's an important question for us to consider. While it's true that all of the pieces are there for a good Hollywood Cinderella story, is there more to this little book? Have you wondered why God chose to include a book in the Bible that doesn't even mention Him? Is it an inspired book of the Bible? Perhaps we should dismiss Esther like Luther and others have suggested. I take up pen and paper, (actually, it's a Mac) to write about this often misunderstood book. My goal is simple; I want to help us to behold our gods, the gods of this world. And to behold our God. I believe Esther exists to help us accomplish both.

I look forward to walking through this "Old" Testament book with you, mining its pages for the often missed glories it contains. But, before we dive in, I think it might be helpful to let the reader know that I hold to three core convictions. These convictions provide a grid that will help you understand how I am approaching this study.

All Of God's Word Is God's Word

All Scripture is breathed out by God and profitable for teaching, for reproof, for correction, and for training in righteousness, that the man of God may be complete, equipped for every good work.

2 Timothy 3:16-17

It is not within the scope of this book to defend the above text. However, there are many great books that do. If you are not convinced that all Scripture is "God-breathed," please put this book down and begin to study this issue for yourself.

If Esther is inspired by God Himself, then certainly this book is useful for instruction. I invite you to dig in and enjoy all of the "breathed-out Word of God," the Old Testament and the New Testament. Early within the pages of the Old Testament, we begin to see a storyline unfold. It is a story of the redemption, mercy, and faithfulness of God. If Esther is part of this redemptive storyline then we might expect it to reveal Christ, the Savior who was to come, and we would do well to explore its glories.

What we have in the Bible is not sixty-six books saying sixty-six different things. It's sixty-six books written by forty plus authors yet, the one Author inspired all sixty-six books. Thus, we should not be surprised to find them all saying one thing, marching to the beat of the same drum, and moving in the same direction. Esther did not drop out of the sky and fall into the Bible. No, it was placed there by God Himself. And since He put it there, we will find it has a purpose for our lives!

All of God's Word is God's Word. We need the book of Esther. The entire Old Testament points to the reality that we have a problem. Humanity is in rebellion against the Creator. The splendor

5

of the Old Testament is how it points us to the fulfillment of the plan of God to redeem fallen man! Which leads us to the next core conviction.

The Book Of Esther Is About Jesus

You might be thinking, *How can a book that never mentions God be about Jesus?* Well, stick around because that is the diamond we are mining. Do you remember when the risen Christ was on the Emmaus Road with his disciples at the end of Luke's gospel? Luke's recording of that conversation and another one that follows is insightful. Listen closely to what he says to them:

"These are my words that I spoke to you while I was still with you, that everything written about me in the Law of Moses and the Prophets and the Psalms must be fulfilled." Then he opened their minds to understand the Scriptures...

Luke 24:44-45

Wow! Did you catch what Jesus said? He's saying that all of the law of Moses, the prophets, and the Psalms are about Himself! He is revealing to His disciples then and now that He is the fulfillment of all the Old Testament. Then He said, "He opened their minds to understand the Scriptures." The word "Scriptures" there didn't include the New Testament; Jesus was talking about the Old Testament. Regarding this, Mike Bullmore writes: "There is probably no passage of Scripture more compelling regarding the Christ-centeredness of Scripture than Luke 24."[5] Jesus also spoke of the Old Testament when He addressed the religious leaders in John.

You search the Scriptures because you think that in them you have eternal life; and it is they that bear witness about me.

John 5:39

---

[5] Bullmore, Mike (2011-08-02). The Gospel and Scripture: How to Read the Bible (The Gospel Coalition Booklets) (Kindle Locations 186-187). Crossway. Kindle Edition.

"For if you believed Moses, you would believe me; for he wrote of me. But if you do not believe his writings, how will you believe my words?"

John 5:46-47

Bryan Chapell states it well in his book *Christ Centered Preaching:* "Every text is predictive of the work of Christ, preparatory for the work of Christ, reflective of the work of Christ, and/or resultant of the work of Christ."[6] That is a helpful approach to God's Word. We are to read Esther, expectantly anticipating to behold Christ. Iain Duguid states:

> The Center of the Old Testament Is Christ. The Old Testament is not primarily a book about ancient history or culture....Centrally, the Old Testament is a book about Christ, and more specifically, about his sufferings and the glories that will follow— that is, it is a book about the promise of a coming Messiah through whose sufferings God will establish his glorious, eternal kingdom.[7]

Isn't that exactly what Jesus said of Himself on the Emmaus road? The wonder of the Old Testament is how it leaves us longing for answers to humanity's greatest problem. How will God remain faithful to His unfaithful people? Will He abandon them due to their belligerent rebellion against Him? Ultimately, Esther and the entire Old Testament's storyline will leave us longing and wondering: *where is God?* Turn the last page of your Old Testament and see its fulfillment in the New Testament as Christ, Immanuel, God-with-us arrives in human flesh! In Christ, all the Old Testament questions are answered. It is in Esther that we find an unlikely savior, holding a position of royalty, fulfilling her role while her Jewish heritage remains veiled. And it is in Christ we find our unlikely Savior. Christ condescended; God became a man while veiling His glory. Esther

---

[6] Chapell, Christ-Centered Preaching: Redeeming the Expository Sermon (Grand Rapids, MI: Baker, 1994), 275.

[7] Duguid, Iain M.; Gaffin, Richard B.; Beale, G. K.; Poythress, Vern M. (2016-04-15). Seeing Christ in All of Scripture: Hermeneutics at Westminster. Theological Seminary Westminster Seminary Press. Kindle Edition.

bore the burden of rescuing her people, facing the uncertainty of death. Whereas, Christ rescued His people through His actual death. The result for the Jews then and Christians today are great celebrations.[8]

Let's walk together as we find there is a fountain of Christ-revealing, gospel-announcing glories tucked within its pages!

Esther Is Relevant To The Days In Which We Now Live

Soon we will see that Esther has something to say to us today. Esther speaks to our comforts, worship, suffering, and how Christians are to handle themselves in the face of opposition or even great danger. Where is God in the pages of Esther and where is God in the story of our lives? Isn't that the ultimate question we have all wondered? Esther contains no burning bushes and no extraordinary, miraculous activity of God. Staffs don't turn into snakes, seas aren't opened, and walls don't come crumbling down in Esther. Does that sound familiar? Have you noticed that divine interventions can seem distant in our lives as well? Are you familiar with the suffering, discouragement, and challenges of living for Christ that leave us all asking, *"Where is God in the story of our lives?"* Is He involved at all in the life of Esther or in our struggles today? The Bible does not shy away from such questions. Indeed, the Psalms are full of laments like this one.

Why, O LORD, do you stand far away? Why do you hide yourself in times of trouble?

Psalm 10:1

These are questions worth wrestling over and contemplating. Let's not be afraid of what we might find; God's Word can handle our questions. What are we to do when our government stands against us?

---

[8] For more on this cross centered / Christ centered themes see: Gregory, Bryan R. (2014-12-30). Inconspicuous Providence: The Gospel According to Esther (Gospel According to the Old Testament) P&R Publishing.
Iain M. Duguid. Esther & Ruth (Reformed Expository Commentary). P&R Publishing

How are we to think when our culture increasingly opposes the Lord and His people? Where is God in the suffering or the decline of morality in a nation? The reality is that our world is not growing in God-honoring morality and the trajectory that we find ourselves on is not encouraging. Evil advances and God is seemingly absent from the pages of our lives. What lies ahead for the church today? Esther's story exists to shape the church in our day to be neither shaken by increasing immorality nor surprised by future suffering. We need to prepare our hearts today for what might be our tomorrow. This readiness is not fatalism. No, we also must pray regularly: "God, please turn the hearts of the people in our day and in our country." We know God is able to do so! However, if God does not choose to turn the tide, my friend, increasing suffering lies ahead for the church.

We need to realize that the Jews were more of a religious minority in the days of Esther than we are in ours. Society was at odds with the Jews in Susa.[9] Likewise, society is at odds with Christians today. Tim Keller asked during a sermon from Esther, "How will the minority live in a culture that opposes them? Is there anything that we might learn as we consider Esther in our day? Do we protest? Do we withdraw? Do we blend in or change our convictions? What does a follower of Christ do when he doesn't know what to do?"[10]

The story of Esther is us and it will increasingly be us given the direction our world seems to be headed. That is why Esther is such a worthwhile book. It has much to offer our 21st-century lives! In Esther, the people of God are living in and under a government that will turn against them. Indeed, the king is going to go so far as to decree the annihilation of all the Jews living in his kingdom. I invite you to join me on this journey that we might behold God and, in so doing, be transformed to be more like Christ.

In picking up this book, I hope that you find it is easy to read. My aim has been to write in an accessible way for everyday people, who are experiencing everyday challenges. It is also my desire that you, the reader, do not read to simply gain information. God's Word

---

[9] Susa is the setting where the book of Esther takes place.

[10] Tim Keller Sermon: www.sermons2.redeemer.com/sermons/silent-sovereignty-god

exists to bring us knowledge that leads to transformation. Lastly, this book was written with the believer in Jesus Christ in mind, though I do hope I have written in such a way that a non-Christian can easily follow along and benefit from its pages as well.

And so, with these core convictions stated, let's begin our study.

Reflections:

- If all of God's Word is God's Word, how might that affect the way you approach a book like Esther?

- As you read the book of Esther, how is Christ beginning to be revealed in the book?

Chapter 1: Understanding Susa

Now in the days of Ahasuerus, the Ahasuerus who reigned from India
to Ethiopia over 127 provinces, in those days when King Ahasuerus
sat on his royal throne in Susa, the citadel....

Esther 1:1-2

Grab your cup of java and let's have that chat mentioned
earlier. Here is the cafe´ question: Why preach a series of messages
on Esther? Why take it one step further and write a book about
Esther? And, if I might be so bold, let me ask you: Why are you
reading a book about Esther? Maybe you are wanting to study and
better understand Esther. Maybe a friend invited you to read this
book, or perhaps, you are drawn to that aforementioned radical
moment of faith when Mordecai exclaims; "for such a time as this."
My purpose in writing this book and thus my prayer for you and me is
two-fold. I write that we might first, behold our gods and second, to
behold our God. To rightly grasp this two-fold purpose, we need to
understand the setting. Where is Susa and what is going on in that
foreign land?

The Backdrop Of Susa

The plot of Esther is one of rising drama. The people of God,
the Jews, were in Susa and they found themselves in quite a mess.
How did they get to Susa and why did they remain there? The events
are unpacked in masterfully crafted storytelling. But it is not a "Once
upon a time" fairytale. It is authentic life and death drama. That
drama builds with a few major players.

It is thought that Esther's name came from the Persian word
for "star" or from the name of the Babylonian love goddess, Ishtar.
Her Hebrew name was "Hadassah" (2:7) which means "myrtle."

Esther, daughter of Abihail, became orphaned and that is how we meet her. Mordecai, Esther's cousin, had been given the responsibility of caring for and raising Esther. Mordecai and Esther were among the Jews who were living far from their ancestor's homeland, Jerusalem. King Ahasuerus was the mighty ruler of the Persian Empire from 486-465 B.C. At the time he was the most powerful man in the world. We are told in Esther 1:1 that the empire extended from India to Ethiopia, 127 provinces. It was a vast and powerful empire that was approximately the same landmass of the United States of America. We might think of Susa as the empire's headquarters. Susa was one of four capitals in Persia, the Washington D.C. of its day. The Citadel in Susa occupied a hilltop in the Persian Empire, modern day Iran.[11]

Obviously, Susa is not Jerusalem! The Jews were a people that were about their land and temple. Land represented God's favor and the temple was where the Lord met with His people. So, we need to ask, what brings us to Esther 1:1?

*...in those days when King Ahasuerus sat on his royal throne **in Susa**, the citadel....*

Esther 1:1-2

The answer is that they found themselves in Susa (Persian Empire), far from home, because the Israelites had been unfaithful to God. Israel had stubbornly turned away from God and, once again, worshiped false gods. They happily rejected God and pursued their rebellion. Instead of turning to the one true God, they went their own way and dismissed Him. As a result, God raised up an army to bring His people back to Him: King Nebuchadnezzar and the Babylonians, the same king we read about in Daniel. The book of Daniel begins:

....In the third year of the reign of Jehoiakim king of Judah, Nebuchadnezzar king of Babylon came to Jerusalem and besieged it.

Daniel 1:1

---

[11] The ESV study Bible provides a very good overview of the purpose, history and themes found in Esther. Crossway Bibles (2009-04-09). ESV Study Bible (Kindle Location 60074). Good News Publishers/Crossway Books. Kindle Edition.

Prior to the famous events that led to the stand off between Nebuchadnezzar and Shadrach, Meshach, and Abednego and a fiery furnace, the Babylonian army completely destroyed Jerusalem, leaving the city and temple as nothing more than piles of rubble. Next, the Babylonians rounded up most of the Israelites and carried them off into slavery for the next 70 years.

Meanwhile, Cyrus, the king of Persia, was also growing in power. Cyrus and the Persians busily built a massive army with the goal of attacking and destroying the Babylonian Empire. Babylon soon fell to the Persians. In doing so, Cyrus inherited the Israelites that the Babylonians had previously captured. However, Cyrus didn't want to keep the Israelites as slaves. Why? Ultimately because God is sovereign and He remained faithful to unfaithful Israel. Therefore, Cyrus decreed that the Jews were free to return to Jerusalem and rebuild the city.

In the first year of Cyrus king of Persia, that the word of the LORD by the mouth of Jeremiah might be fulfilled, the LORD stirred up the spirit of Cyrus king of Persia, so that he made a proclamation throughout all his kingdom and also put it in writing:

"Thus says Cyrus king of Persia: The LORD, the God of heaven, has given me all the kingdoms of the earth, and he has charged me to build him a house at Jerusalem, which is in Judah. Whoever is among you of all his people, may his God be with him, and let him go up to Jerusalem, which is in Judah, and rebuild the house of the LORD...

Ezra 1:1-3

Many Israelites packed their bags and returned to rebuild the city walls and the temple. However, not everyone made the journey back to Jerusalem. The events in Esther took place about 50 years after Cyrus released the Jews to return home. Esther and Mordecai were among the Jews who remained and did not return for the rebuilding program. Why did they stay back? We can only speculate. Perhaps some Jews remained in Susa because Persia is all they had ever known. After all, who wants to return to Jerusalem and rebuild? The city walls were a pile of rocks; the temple was in shambles and life was difficult back in Jerusalem. Rebuilding Jerusalem required hard labor while life in Susa was comparatively easy. We all typically choose the path of least resistance.

> *Now there was a Jew in Susa the citadel whose name was Mordecai, the son of Jair, son of Shimei, son of Kish, a Benjaminite, who had been carried away from Jerusalem among the captives carried away with Jeconiah king of Judah, whom Nebuchadnezzar king of Babylon had carried away.*

Esther 2:5-6

Now, I personally believe that Esther and Mordecai needed to pack their bags and catch the first train out of Susa. They belonged in Jerusalem with the worshiping community of God. God had provided a means for them to return, yet they lingered in Susa. There were three separate journeys where many Jews returned to rebuild their lives in Jerusalem. It is likely that Esther took place between the first and the second return.[12]

Believer, this world is not your home. I Peter 2:11 tells us we are "sojourners and exiles" in this world; we are citizens of heaven. We have grown comfortable in this world, our "Susa." It is where we have grown up and it's all we have known. After all, being a disciple who seeks to follow Christ among the worshiping community of God is hard! We, like Esther and Mordecai, desire to take the path of least resistance. Many avoid the worshiping community of God in our day, not unlike Mordecai and Esther did in theirs. Let Esther be a word of warning to us. Susa is a reminder for the Jews that this city is not their home. Christian, we are pilgrims in this world; this world is not your home!

God provided for the Jews by raising up a pagan king. It was God who raised Cyrus, brought him to power, and now through him decreed that the Jews could return to Jerusalem. The Lord keeps His promises. Behold the faithfulness, mercy, and grace of God! Esther certainly would have known the stories of how her ancestors had been dragged from their homes and thrown into slavery. This decree is worthy of a celebration! Cyrus decreed because the Lord had already

---

[12] To learn more about Cyrus' decree and the return of the Jews to Jerusalem, refer to the books of Ezra and Nehemiah

covenanted! Imagine those Jews who had returned as they gathered together again as the worshiping community of God. At the same time, others remained and stayed under the self-proclaimed god: Ahasuerus. This contrast then shapes the background to our story. Esther is about gods and God.

Haman The Agagite

*After these things King Ahasuerus promoted **Haman the Agagite**, the son of Hammedatha, and advanced him and set his throne above all the officials who were with him.*

Esther 3:1

In Esther 3 we are introduced to Haman the Agagite. The author's repeated reference to Haman's Agagite background provides the backdrop to understanding the rising conflict in Esther. Haman was quickly promoted into positions of power and that is where we find the building tensions between Haman *the Agagite* and Mordecai *the Jew*. Mordecai was stubborn in his refusal to pay homage to Haman. As a result, Haman wanted Mordecai and all his ancestors dead. As we approach the book of Esther it is important that we understand that there is a reason for all this. These guys have a history!

Actually, we could say that the book of Esther has been 1,000+ years in the making. For this mutual contempt to make sense, we must look back to the Jews exodus from Egypt. That's right. We are talking about Moses and the Jews' deliverance from slavery that we read about in the book of Exodus. When the Jews left Egypt, the first people they encountered in the desert was the Amalekites (Exodus 17:8-16). It is here that the Esther story actually begins. Genesis 36 shows us that the Amalekites were descendants of Esau. As the newly freed Jews stumbled into the desert, the Amalekites seized the opportunity and savagely attacked God's chosen people.

Due to the attack of this savage attack on the Jews, God cursed the Amalekites. "Why," you ask? Well, in attacking the Jews, the Amalekites stood in the way of God's covenant promises that He had made with Abraham and His people in Genesis 12. An argument could be made that the Amalekites stood in the way of our salvation. Their opposition was not with the Jews; they were opposing the very character of God, His promises, and His redemption of fallen man! The question regarding this attack in the desert is this: Will God remain faithful to His covenant promise made to Abraham? If the Amalekites defeat God's people there in the desert, God is not faithful and His promises have become meaningless. That is what's at stake in the desert battle. God made a covenant with Israel, the very people that the Amalekites are fighting were the promised people of God!

Then the LORD said to Moses, "Write this as a memorial in a book and recite it in the ears of Joshua, that I will utterly blot out the memory of Amalek from under heaven."

Exodus 17:14

"Remember what Amalek did to you on the way as you came out of Egypt, how he attacked you on the way when you were faint and weary, and cut off your tail, those who were lagging behind you, and he did not fear God. Therefore when the LORD your God has given you rest from all your enemies around you, in the land that the LORD your God is giving you for an inheritance to possess, you shall blot out the memory of Amalek from under heaven; you shall not forget.

Deuteronomy 25:17-19

The opportunity to carry out the above fell on Israel's first king, Saul (I Samuel 15:2-3). However, Saul arrogantly assumed that God's plans needed some adjustments. He knew what God commanded and yet, in his pride, he determined a "better" path for Israel. Saul spared Agag, king of the Amalekites (I Samuel 15:7-9) which brought about God's displeasure (I Samuel 11, 26, 28:18). King Saul thought little of the Lord's commands and thought much of himself. He did not fear the Lord. Saul, like you and I, had an awe problem. His disregard for God's clear commands was directly related to his lack of awe of God, replaced by a reverent awe of himself. Paul Tripp writes explaining Saul's and our "awe wrongedness" which he calls "AWN." AWN is our lack of AWE of God. AWN does not awe God; it's too consumed with self to do so. We think we know what is best. Knowing God's commands, we figure we'll go our own way and do our own thing.

> *Saul acted like he was in charge and had the right to set his own rules, and because he did, he took plunder for himself rather than destroying it all as God had commanded. To make matters worse, rather than admit his AWN-induced disobedience, he blamed the people of Israel. The prophet Samuel uncovered Saul's actual motives: 'For rebellion is as the sin of divination, and presumption is as iniquity and idolatry' (v. 23). You see, Saul's problem was not that he disagreed with God's strategy for dealing with the Amalekites. No, Saul had a heart problem. His heart was captured more by the awe of physical things than by God. AWN caused him to crave what God had forbidden and to rebel against God's clear commands. So God, in a clear display of who was in charge and who had the authority to set the rules, turned his back on Saul and his reign. AWN is not just shockingly blind and morally wrong, it is also inescapably self-destructive.[13]*

For this reason, the author of Esther is providing us important information when he tells us that Haman was an Agagite and that Mordecai was a Jew. To say these two men don't get along is a grand understatement! They have a history of deeply rooted hostilities towards each other. Esther takes place approximately 550 years after Saul's disobedience. However, for Haman and Mordecai the sting and the spilling of blood is still fresh.

This hostility explains why Mordecai refused to pay homage to Haman. The revealing of this tension underpinning the situation helps us understand why Haman is driven to bring an end to not only Mordecai but to all the Jews. Additionally, much irony runs through the book. Haman rose to be a man of great power, becoming the second in command to the king himself. What did Haman do with that

---

[13] Tripp, Paul David (2015-10-14). Awe: Why It Matters for Everything We Think, Say, and Do (pp. 34-35). Crossway. Kindle Edition.

power? Well, of course, he did what any good Amalekite would do. He viewed his position and power to be an opportunity to destroy the Jews. We could even say that he viewed his role to be a "for such a time as this..." moment. Ironically, it is a *"for such a time as this..."* moment but not for Haman the Agagite. Rather, it was a moment sovereignly orchestrated by God for the Jews.[14]

This ongoing Amalekite/Jewish conflict is an important theme throughout the book of Esther. When great powers rose up to eliminate God's people they were not simply attacking the Jews. No, they attacked God himself and the covenant He had made with His people. God's covenant promises were what was at stake in Esther. Will God's people and His promises be completely wiped out? Nothing less than the character of God, the faithfulness of God, is on the line in Esther.

A Review:

- After the Exodus, the Jews were attacked by the Amalekites in the desert. (Exodus 17)

- Saul became the first King of Israel (1 Samuel 13:1). He foolishly disobeyed God by sparing Agag, the King of the Amalekites (I Samuel 15).

- The Babylonians under King Nebuchadnezzar destroyed Jerusalem and carried the Jews into captivity in 586 B.C.

- The Persians under Cyrus conquered the Babylonians in 539 B.C.

- Cyrus issued a decree allowing the captive Jews to return and rebuild Jerusalem.

- Esther takes place approximately 50 years after Cyrus' decree.

---

[14] I recommend John McArthur for a brief history of Esther: http://www.gty.org/resources/bible-introductions/MSB17/esther
For a more in depth study of Esther see: Michael V. Fox. Character and Ideology in the Book of Esther

Reflections:

- If you were living in Esther's day, what do you think you would have done? Would you have returned to Jerusalem where much hard work laid ahead or would you have remained in Susa?

- Prayerfully consider how you may have grown overly comfortable living in this world.

Chapter 2: The Glory Of A god, And The Glory Of God

"The promise of glory is the promise, almost incredible and only possible by the work of Christ, that some of us, that any of us... shall please God... to be loved by God, not merely pitied, but delighted in as an artist delights in his work or a father in a son – it seems impossible, a weight or burden of glory which our thoughts can hardly sustain. But so it is."

C.S. Lewis

I guess one might say that Esther is about king Ahasuerus, his kingdom, and his glory. That is, after all, how the book begins. However, Esther is about another King, King Jesus, His Kingdom, and His glory. One king makes a grand show by displaying his extravagant wealth and power. The other King never appears on the written page and yet it is His great power that is gloriously displayed.

The author of Esther wants us to take note as these verses go to great lengths to deliberately display and flaunt power and wealth right down to the goblets and curtains.[15]

*Now in the days of Ahasuerus, the Ahasuerus who reigned from India to Ethiopia over **127 provinces,** in those days when King Ahasuerus sat on his royal throne in Susa, the citadel, in the third year of his reign he gave a feast for all his officials and servants. The army of Persia and Media and the nobles and governors of the provinces were before him, **while he showed the riches of his royal glory and the splendor and pomp of his greatness for many days... 180 days. And***

---

[15] The author of the book of Esther is anonymous.

*when these days were completed, the king gave for all the people present in Susa the citadel, both great and small, a feast lasting for seven days in the court of the garden of the king's palace. **There were white cotton curtains and violet hangings fastened with cords of fine linen and purple to silver rods and marble pillars, and also couches of gold and silver on a mosaic pavement of porphyry, marble, mother-of-pearl and precious stones. Drinks were served in golden vessels, vessels of different kinds, and the royal wine was lavished according to the bounty of the king.** And drinking was according to this edict: "There is no compulsion." For the king had given orders to all the staff of his palace to do as each man desired. Queen Vashti also gave a feast for the women....*

Esther 1:1-9

Behold Our gods

Land

Everything in these first nine verses is intended to show us the glory of a king. Appearances matter in the book of Esther! The mentioning of land shows the vast power of the king. His reign is expansive, extending from India to Ethiopia, over 127 provinces!

> *At the height of its power after the conquest of Egypt, the empire encompassed approximately 3 million square miles spanning three continents: Asia, Africa and Europe. At its greatest extent, the empire included the modern territories of Iran, Turkey, parts of Central Asia, Pakistan, Thrace and Macedonia, much of the Black Sea coastal regions, Afghanistan, Iraq, northern Saudi Arabia, Jordan, Israel, Lebanon, Syria, and all significant population centers of ancient Egypt as far west as Libya.[16]*

These details are provided for us to stand back and think, *whoa, Ahasuerus is a powerful king! Look at all the land he ruled; behold His glory, there was no one quite like him.* His vast empire

---

[16] http://www.bible-history.com/maps/04-persian-empire.html

21

was a seemingly infinite display of the king's power. At the time, Ahasuerus was the most powerful man in the world and the book of Esther goes to great lengths to make that reality clear to us.

Throne

In those days, king Ahasuerus sat on his royal throne in Susa. This throne would have been built on the highest point so that all the common people could look up and see the king's vast display of power and wealth. A note regarding the throne: one did not approach it lightly or without risking one's life. As we will come to see, commoners were not to appear before the king's throne!

Military Power

The 180-day event that introduced the book of Esther likely included a gathering of military officials. The Persian army was the dominating force in Esther's day. It is speculated that the military leaders had gathered in Susa to strategize Greece's ultimate defeat. Aware of their vast and expanding powers, they presumed their enemy would soon be destroyed. The smell of the victory that was soon to be theirs hung in the air. Thus, the atmosphere of Esther 1:1-9 was celebratory.

Prior to Ahasuerus' rule, Persia's enemy, the Greeks, had been a problem for king Darius. The Persian army under king Darius had been defeated and humiliated by the weaker, smaller armies of Greece. As a result, Darius rebuilt a massive army to exact revenge on Greece. However, he died and the unfinished business fell to his son. This son of Darius rose in power to avenge his father. He was bloodthirsty and hungry for war with Greece. Darius' son was none other than Xerxes. Xerxes the Great, a.k.a. king Ahasuerus! The mantle had been passed; plans were being made, strategies of war were being devised and though the battles had not yet begun, Persia was already basking in victory.

Lavish Parties

The Esther story wastes no time dropping us right into the feast with the military brass, leaders, and highly esteemed guests. It was the gathering place for the rich and famous. The common man could look up to the Citadel and see the flocks of people that were crowding into the palace for the banquet. Some estimate that upwards of 15,000 people were gathered at this 180-day banquet. Additionally, a seven-day festival was provided for all the people of Susa, great and small alike. Lastly, queen Vashti also threw a feast for the women.

The king was so thorough in his display of power and control that an edict was issued that all were to *"drink without compulsion."* Just imagine this 180-day party, complete with golden goblets, elegant curtains, golden couches, and an endless supply of alcohol. Why does the book present such minutia of information? This exhibition of grandeur and benevolence was provided for our benefit. The author is telling us, "look at the king, gaze at his splendor, behold his glory!"

Why write and preach about Esther? Because Esther is us. Have you noticed that our world is consumed with what consumed the king's honored guests? Ours is a world that lusts for this party. Our culture and our hearts long for this Susa, its king, his wealth, and the parties he threw.

Esther 1 is not as distant as it might first seem. Our flesh loves all that makes up the first nine verses of the book. How much money was being released from the king's coffers into that 180-day party? The 21st century looks oddly similar to Persia. The more money that is dropped on an event the more we become entranced. Like a pathetic insect irresistibly drawn to a street light, we gaze, mouth wide open, stunned by the glory of it all; we can't seem to get enough. Grab the cameras; upload the pictures, capture a selfie with the king and post it to the timeline. How many "Likes" will I get? Perhaps it will go viral. Wealth, beauty, and power are on display and our culture longs to be in the middle of it all.

Beauty

Physical appearances play a major role in Esther. The book of Esther shifts quickly from displaying the vast wealth of the king to displaying the king's wife, Vashti. Additionally, the king had many wives, most of whom were a part of the royal harem. The harem was a designated part of the palace that housed all of the women the king had set aside. Women in those days were greatly mistreated. Consequently, Queen Vashti was not a wife like we might think of today. The book of Esther introduces the reader to Vashti as nothing more than another part of the king's exhibition. The king displayed golden vessels, gold and silver couches, marble pillars and attractive women. Sadly, the king's power and glory were made evident through his dominance and control over many women. The more women and wives the king gathered, the greater his power and glory were displayed. Unsurprisingly, the role that beauty played is well noted in the book of Esther.

This guy Ahasuerus had all the stuff that our hearts often long for. Ahasuerus was considered to be a god, this false deity is still reflected in today's society. It's what sells magazines and drives the ad nauseum prime time drivel. We bottle up verses 1-9 and call it "reality TV." We long to see the exhibition and extravagant glamor of the rich and famous. Throw in some beauty and you have a blockbuster. Social media promotes it; Hollywood exalts it; we buy it. Picture this Ahasuerus living today: he'd be on all the talk shows. Everyone would want to listen in to what this powerful man had to say. Even more popular would be the beauty contest to determine the new and improved queen. This ultimate Miss Universe pageant would dominate the ratings in our day. After all, he's the eligible bachelor god and king! What single woman in the kingdom wouldn't have wanted to be attached to him? The king had more land, money, and power than any of his competitors. "Xerxes, Son of Darius, photographed as he exits to his Learjet with women on both arms!" We love this stuff. It captures our gaze and we lust for all that it offers.

The point of verses 1-9 is to behold these gods, small "g". This lavish description intentionally puts the king's glory on display. We are led to think: *wow, look at the king, see his wealth, behold his glory!* People were impressed then and we are engrossed now as we behold these same gods in our present-day.

Isn't that the way our gods/idols work? Different gods ensnare each of us but, whatever god it is, our hunger for it is insatiable. None of us are immune to the enticement of the false god!

What brings a man to rush into an adulterous affair that will wreck his marriage, embitter his children and destroy his career? False gods do; they promise life and deliver death. What presses a person to push aside his or her hatred of the drug that rules them? Enslaved to the pills, he or she returns to that place of dreaded existence. The promise of relief from overwhelming stress, the desire to forget reality, the longing to dismiss problems from the mind all cause us to run to all sorts of idols: drink, drugs, affairs, tv, and a thousand others call for our allegiance. Our hearts are what John Calvin called "a perpetual factory of idols."[17] The shiny yet shallow bling of the false gods quickly fade. These false gods lie to us. The promise fails; relief is fleeting; the emptiness remains. As the hangover lurks, the realities we seek to escape will wait and return with a vengeance. The idol drops us! Our gods make false guarantees of freedom but never deliver on the promise. They cannot do so. In contrast, Christ has given us new life in Him! In Christ, we can repent and turn to Him who has set us free from the madness of the idol factory.

I will sprinkle clean water on you, and you shall be clean from all your uncleannesses, and from all your idols I will cleanse you. And I will give you a new heart, and a new spirit I will put within you. And I will remove the heart of stone from your flesh and give you a heart of flesh.

Ezekiel 36:25-26

Behold our gods, plural and with a small "g". This is why we have the book of Esther! See Ahasuerus then and now. See the gods of this world that seek to capture our affections. The gods are like the sand we hold in our hands, promising something (and even temporarily satisfying us) but always slipping through our fingers and falling to the ground. It's gone, just as Ahasuerus and all his great display of wealth and power are gone today. Behold our gods, Esther is an opportunity for us to repent.

---

[17] John Calvin, Institutes, I.II.8

Behold our God

The book of Esther exists to help us to behold our God, singular with a capital "G". I mentioned that there is much irony within the pages of Esther. Perhaps the fact that God is not named in Esther is the single greatest aspect of irony in the book. As students of God's Word, how do we approach a book that is in the Bible that never mentions God? Was this an oversight by the author? Where is God and who is God in this book? Are you ready for the irony? He is never mentioned so that we might see Him more. That's right. In studying Esther, we're to see how the king went to great lengths to display his grandeur. All the land, gold, and power was to be seen, while our God, the King, remained behind the scenes. Though Esther never mentions the glory of God, it was His glory, not Ahasuerus' that we are to behold. All that power and wealth was simply on loan to the earthly king from *the* King. Ahasuerus died; his rule was temporary, while the King who remained unmentioned rules eternally! The hand of God was clearly at work and entirely in control from start to finish. By not naming Him, His glory is brightly displayed. Mordecai and Esther never referred to God, no prayer was heard, no worship was lifted. Nevertheless, God is God even when He is undisclosed.

God remains God even when He's not on our lips (Esther 2:10). Indeed, He is God whether you believe in Him or not. That is the glory of our God. God is not glorious because *we* speak His name. He is glorious because that is what He is. He *is* glorious! While king Ahasuerus ruled a vast empire, it was God who created that empire and breathed life into the king! There is no comparison between these two kingdoms. The Persian kingdom is a small slice of all that God had made. With God's glory in view, this supposed display of vast power and wealth is appropriately sized. As I re-read verses 1-9 I think: *Is that all? This guy who thinks himself to be a god, is that the extent of his glory and power?* He had attained all that wealth and yet he was so small that he could do nothing with it beyond his few ordained years of life. While ruling over a vast empire, we will soon see, his rule is out of control within the walls of his own palace. The glory of that king ironically displayed the glory of *the* King.

Who is God in the book of Esther and what is the display of His glory? The unnamed God is the God of mercy who rescued unfaithful Israel. He is the faithful God who kept His covenant. He is the God of grace who brought that grace to the undeserving. He is the Sovereign One who used Ahasuerus, Haman, Mordecai, and Esther to usher in His sovereign plan. The glory of the King is such that His redemption plan would not be thwarted due to a reckless king and an ungodly government. Esther is a display of Proverbs 21:1 *"The king's heart is a stream of water in the hand of the Lord; he turns it wherever he will."* The prophet Isaiah speaks of the glory of God as he considers the nations. *Behold, the nations are like a drop from a bucket, and are accounted as the dust on the scales; behold, he takes up the coastlands like fine dust.* Behold your God in Esther as He powerfully accomplishes His sovereign purposes.

Now, you might not believe in the sovereign hand of God. Nevertheless, your belief in God's sovereignty does not change the fact that God is God. God was undeniably at work in both the unbelievers and believers in the book of Esther. It was the Lord our God who was orchestrating His sovereign plan to rescue the Jews who had been unfaithful, stubbornly rebelling against Him. Additionally, God was at work in an ungodly king and the secular government. Behold your God! Esther is a book that unpacks the mercy and faithfulness of God to unfaithful Israel. God will have a people! If you are a believer in Jesus Christ, you are a part of that people!

We miss the mark when we think the book is about Ahasuerus, that "he's the king and it's about his glory." Or that it's about Haman, that we are being told: "don't be like evil Haman!" Or that it is about Esther and moralism: "let's fast, for such a time as this." Even though we certainly do learn something from each of these individuals, ultimately Esther is about the One who is never mentioned! What a beautiful and glorious irony! Esther is about the King, capital "K". It is about the One who is not named and is not on the lips of His people.

This mercy is a glory worthy to behold! He is actively at work redeeming you and me. Even when this world doesn't name Him; or when we don't see His hand at work, we're to read Esther and see that God continued to move among His people. Powerful people and mighty governments will come and go but God remains. The King

27

who is not to be found on the pages of the book of Esther is to be found on the throne, ruling over all!

God Himself created Esther and thus He is the one who made her beautiful. By no accident, He made her a Jew. God gave her life and had her to be born in Persia, living under the care of Mordecai. God did all that, the God that was not named. God is a God who has been on a mission since the fall of man in the garden of Eden. We are to read Esther and see that He's saving His people then and He continues to save His people today. Map your redemptive story line right into Esther. Esther's story is every believer's heritage.

The stakes are high in Esther. We must not belittle this book by assigning it to be little more than a good moral story: *go and be like Esther.* The events in Susa are a threat to God's eternal decrees and His character. Will God have a people and will He redeem fallen man? Whose decree will stand in Esther, and which King will endure?

How big is your God? How big is your understanding of His providence? Do you have a small view of God? *Yeah, He's remotely involved. Sometimes He's participating. I am sure He has some part in bringing me to saving faith...* Do you hold the view that he winds up the clock, takes a step back, and then lets it wind down? Or, is God... God? Is the King ruling both then and now?

Without mentioning God, the book of Esther holds to a big view of God. God is on His throne and He's involved in our lives moment by moment. He breathed life into us, placed us in a home, a family and, a set of circumstances. You live in a neighborhood and work in a cubicle. He placed you there because He's about redeeming the lives of those who don't have His name on their lips. He has saved you and now through you, He's saving others.

Whatever land you call home and whatever government is over you, God did that! What are we to think when the economy is difficult? What are we to do when the President is not the one of our choosing? Where are we to turn when suffering surrounds us? The book of Esther helps us to turn to the eternal God, who is reigning over all these temporary circumstances.

For the saving of lives, God raised up secular kings like Cyrus, Darius, and Ahasuerus! While we complain about our first world problems, God continues to work. He is doing something greater than ensuring that you and I have a nice, comfortable nest egg at the time of our retirement. He is up to something more enduring than your best life now; He redeemed His people then in Susa and He's redeeming a people today!

There was a god in Susa and there is a God in Heaven. The god of Susa is long gone. His rule and reign are no more. Our God left His heavenly throne and came to walk among the commoners. Behold the glory of *the* King who took on human flesh, died for the commoners, and rose from the grave. Today, He has ascended and He is, once again, seated on His throne! His Kingdom is forever and we will, one day, see Him seated on that throne. God did something eternal in Esther. Read Esther and behold your God!

Reflection:

- Prior to reading this chapter, how would you describe the purpose of the book of Esther?

- Pause and prayerfully ask God to reveal Himself to you that you might "behold our God!"

Chapter 3: **God, Where Are You?**

"Trying to figure out God is like trying to catch a fish in the Pacific Ocean with an inch of dental floss."

Matt Chandler, The Explicit Gospel

"What are you really living for? It's crucial to realize that you either glorify God, or you glorify something or someone else. You're always making something look big."

Ken Sande

I remember being a vibrant 25-year-old, seemingly invincible and a picture of health... or so I thought. I had been married for four years and we were anticipating the joyful birth of our first born. Life was moving forward smoothly until one day when the unexpected happened.

It's not the norm when a doctor calls you at work. I still remember that morning, alone in my office, when the secretary announced that I had a phone call on line one. She stated, "I think he said he's your doctor." It was my doctor; he was requesting to see both myself and my wife, Kim. "Sure," I said, "Do you want me to make an appointment for one day this week?" "No," came the reply on the other end, "would it be possible for you and your wife to come by the office now?" Somewhat stuttering and quite a bit confused, I answered, "Yeah, I think we should be able to do that."

Thinking about that day 20+ years later is still very surreal. It was on that unplanned afternoon that I was told I had cancer,

Hodgkin's disease. "Hodgkin's disease, what's that?" we fearfully asked the doctor. We had no category for how our lives were about to change. We did not launch into that year imagining that we might want to move from our home and live in the American Cancer Center's Winn Dixie Lodge.[18] We had no idea that it would become necessary so that we might be a few minutes away from Shands Hospital in Gainesville, Florida. We never dreamed of a day where the halls of Shands Cancer Center would become our home away from home. At times I think I can still smell it, the stench of the sterile environment. Nothing smells as it ought when one's life is being snuffed out via chemo drugs. How do you make plans and prepare for days like that? You don't. Three weeks into chemotherapy, our daughter Kaylee was born, bringing such joy in the midst of indescribable turmoil and uncertainty. The birth of life collided with the possibility of death. Nothing could be more deflating than chemo and nothing could be more uplifting than our firstborn! Cancer lows were lower than we thought we could endure and the birth of our first child provided highs that were higher than we had ever imagined.

After a season of chemotherapy, I began 28 sessions of radiation therapy. I thought chemo was undesirable until I met his cousin, radiation! I remember receiving my first radiation treatment to the stomach. I had already been radiated in the neck and chest. Burnt to a crisp, it was time to radiate the abdomen area. All the previous pain I had experienced and all the warnings of my medical team did not prepare me for that day. For months on end, uncontrollable heaving became a normal part of the day; the car, the yard, the parking lot, and everywhere else I went. I traveled with a bag, always pulling into the parking lot on the lookout for a little privacy. There were days I thought I was going to die and days when the thought of dying seemed like a welcomed relief. Chemo and radiation had beat me like a defeated boxer. Against the ropes, my body had had enough; I was unable to continue. Seven days short of finishing the prescribed therapy, my doctor told me: "We have decided your body needs to recover. We believe it is no longer safe for us to continue as planned. We are going to stop any further treatments." I walked out of Shands hospital in Gainesville, Florida

---

[18] We remain grateful for the Winn Dixie Hope Lodge! https://www.cancer.org/treatment/support-programs-and-services/patient-lodging/hope-lodge/gainesville/about-our-facility.html

thanking God that the radiation had finally come to an end. I had no idea what the future held but at that moment, it didn't seem to matter. All I knew is that, for now, I was done with radiation and chemotherapy.

Thankfully, our little family trudged through it. My body began to heal and eventually, I returned to a normal life. However, it had been mentioned that a future child was an unlikely prospect for us. The toll on my body from the therapies was significant. We soon learned that the medical community does not determine future children. Two years later, we had our second child and we went on to have a third and then a fourth! The tears still flow considering those days and all God has brought us through. Thank you God for Kaylee, Tyler, Timothy, and Tanner! They are each a unique joy and blessing from the Lord!

Life moved forward as things settled and became a bit more "normal". Perhaps my only annoyance was that life seemed to be moving too fast. Cancer was behind us when we met something that would somehow exceed the challenges of chemo and radiation. I began to get sick and the doctors assumed cancer had returned. It was a devastating year or so of endless tests, labs, CAT scans, MRI's, PET scans, poking, and probing. On and on it went. Eventually, I was diagnosed with Crohn's disease. Crohn's would become my nightmare for the next decade.

The above is the short version of most of my adult life. I am not complaining and I have close friends who are experiencing far worse. But I recount those events because they are the events in my life that provided the right amount of suffering to press out the question, in raw and honest moments of despair and utter uncertainty; "God, where are you?"

Thankfully, by God's grace, I often slept with some level of relief from the pain. Even with great amounts of insomnia, a side affect of my friend Prednisone, night time was grace. Odd how sleepless nights became my moments of greatest relief. I thanked God for those non-sleeping yet peaceful nights. I even began enjoying the quiet nights of extended reading that the drug provided. On the other hand, the morning haunted me on a regular basis. As I would finally grab a few hours of sleep only to awake to the realization that the peace and joy of a pain-free night was over and it was time to clothe myself in the pain of my disease. It was a daily smack in the face, a dose of reality. *"Good morning Tim..... you are gravely ill."* And some of those mornings included crying out to God, "God, where are you?"

And, while at times God *seemed* distant, the one thing I learned the most during the years of pain, surgeries, endless vomiting, and another Thanksgiving meal apart from my family, was that God had not left me. He was not distant! Our God is always near. So near, that he was in the very storms that we faced. Seemingly alone, we were never alone. He was in the pain, the loss of weight (dropping down to 110lbs), the tears, and even with me in my anger and despairing cries. Charles Spurgeon says it well: "I have learned to kiss the wave that slams me into the rock of ages." At the time of this writing, I am no longer suffering in my diseases. I like to jokingly say that, "I am the picture of health." While that may not be true, I am twenty-three years cancer free and approaching six years free from any symptoms of Crohn's disease. Still, I am gradually learning to "kiss that wave." I am a slow learner, thankfully our God is a patient God.[19]

Where is God in Esther? Has He deserted His people? Have you experienced moments where you felt abandoned by God? Moments that left you wondering, accusing, or asking the question that you don't want to ask, but eventually do in the dark night of the soul: "God, where are you?" Sometimes, all we have to do is watch a little news, take a look at our government, or observe the moral decline of our nation. We see the decadence, where godlessness is exalted and God's Word is mocked. Today's news feed includes yet another post of Christians who were beheaded by ISIS, refugees on the run with nowhere to go, human trafficking, and babies being

---

[19] Thank you to my amazing, God-loving wife. She held my hand and loved me when sickness had left me unlovable. Her faith was unwavering through it all. Jesus was and is her Rock! Thank you Kim, I love you so much! To both our our parents: Thank you for always praying and always offering to help. To my brother and best friend, Jeff, thanks for your friendship! To my dad who drove me the nearly three hours, one way, back and forth from Gainesville - I don't know how many times, thank you! To Kaylee, my newborn daughter at the time, thanks for cooing and smiling up at your sick dad! To many of you, family and friends, who prayed and sent us financial help with the mountain of bills - thanks to all of you!

aborted and sold for body parts. Is there no end to the depths of our corruptions?

Perhaps you have spent more time at funerals than weddings. You might not have any kids or maybe your child was born with a severe disability. Your story might include the agony of an unexpected death, a painful divorce, or the hurt of loneliness. All of these scenarios and a thousand more cry out: "God, where are you?" We live in a fallen world and that means suffering is part of the human existence until Christ returns. The point of Esther is to help us to behold our God in the midst of this fallen world and in the face of suffering. Where is God? While Ahasuerus rules from his royal throne, we are left wondering: *Has God abandoned His throne?* Where was God in Esther and where was God when I would wake in the morning dressed in the pain and uncertainty of my disease? The question is valid; God can handle it. Perhaps this same question was asked by God's people in Susa as they saw the power and wealth of the pagan king. "God where are you?" Isn't that the question we should ask of the book of Esther and isn't that the question that is still being asked today?

Fallen Man

What we see in Esther 1 is a display of the fallenness of man. On the one hand, we wrestle to see God on the written page while on the other, the depravity of man jumps off the page. God is seemingly nowhere present and depravity is seemingly omnipresent.

In the midst of the opulent festivities we are told that the king was "merry with wine" (Esther 1:10). It seems that he had too much to drink because this is what brought about another foolish decree. The king commanded seven of his royal eunuchs to bring his prized possession as the grand finale display. Queen Vashti was to make an appearance. First, the king displayed his power and wealth. Now, he desired to show off his beautiful queen (1:10-11). Vashti was to put on her royal attire and parade herself before the drunken crowd. Her beauty was such that we are told that "...she was lovely to look at." Drunken men awaited to see the trophy wife of the king. Ahasuerus would not disappoint them. Vashti was treated like a piece of property, another part of the show, not unlike the curtains, couches, and goblets. Vashti existed for the king's pleasure and the further display of his glory. Clearly, in the midst of this drunkenness, the king had no regard or respect for his wife, the queen. Consequently, Vashti rejected the king's command, thus publicly humiliating the king! Didn't she know that the whole point of the festivities was to display power, wealth, and beauty that is only deserving of a king? Instead, she publicly snubbed the king in front of all his powerful, drunken guests.

Wow! Can you imagine all that Vashti had gone through to bring her to this point? We can be certain that much has led up to this royal rebuffing of the king. Vashti was not thrilled about the prospect of being paraded in front of the king and his drunken buddies. Now, she was no fool. She knew that to stand up to the king and publicly humiliate the most powerful man in the world was not without its consequences. Was she looking at a death sentence? Certainly, that was not beyond her thoughts of what might be possible by the reckless king. It is here that we begin to see the unraveling of the character of Ahasuerus as he burned with anger.

Then Memucan said in the presence of the king and the officials, "Not only against the king has Queen Vashti done wrong, but also against all the officials and all the peoples who are in all the provinces of King Ahasuerus. For the queen's behavior will be made known to all women, causing them to look at their husbands with contempt, since they will say, 'King Ahasuerus commanded Queen Vashti to be brought before him, and she did not come.' This very day the noble women of Persia and Media who have heard of the queen's behavior will say the same to all the king's officials, and there will be contempt and wrath in plenty. If it please the king, let a royal order go out from him, and let it be written among the laws of the Persians and the Medes so that it may not be repealed, that Vashti is never again to come before King Ahasuerus. And let the king give her royal position to another who is better than she. So when the decree made by the king is proclaimed throughout all his kingdom, for it is vast, all women will give honor to their husbands, high and low alike." This advice pleased the king and the princes, and the king did as Memucan proposed. He sent letters to all the royal provinces, to every province in its own script and to every people in its own language, that every man be master in his own household...

Esther 1:16-20

Panic rushed through the castle as the drunken crowd heard of the royal dissing. The king could not allow this disobedience to go unpunished. After all, actions as such might spread and soon all the women would follow that "unruly woman." What would the king do? How would he respond to this royal snubbing? The pressure mounted as all eyes were upon him, awaiting his reaction to this unthinkable act.

All The King's Men

The king, the most powerful man in the world, was humiliated. He must respond swiftly with a display of strength, showing Vashti, his distinguished guests, and all the women in the empire that he was a man of power.

Before the king acted, he consulted with his advisors. They were tasked with determining what must be done to save the king's face and keep all of Persia and Medes from all out *wife*-anarchy! What would the empire think if someone was allowed to get away with such disrespect? The show of gold curtains and marble pillars were at risk. War with Greece can wait; we have a colossal issue before us! Tossing the war maps to the ground, they began to strategize how to eliminate widespread husband-dissing.

Humor cuts through the written page as the king who seemingly rules the world has a wife beyond that rule. This controlling man has lost control. To regain it, a swift and comprehensive solution was offered. In the end, He sent Vashti packing. And, herein, we find side-splitting irony. Vashti was unwilling to be in the presence of the king. The king's wise counselors determined that the king should banish her from his presence. Yes, you read that right! Imagine the child who sneaks a cookie from the cookie jar banished to his bedroom with the cookie jar in hand! That is what was happening in Susa. Her punishment for rejecting the king was the very thing she desired.

Following the "out with the old and in with the new" mentality, Ahasuerus eventually announced there would be a new queen in Susa. He made it clear that one does not cross the king and get away with it! Iain Duguid writes, "The law might be able to compel people to drink as they wished, but it could not ultimately compel the king's wife to be treated as a sex object. A mere woman stood up and said 'No!' and the empire was powerless to enforce its will. The mouse had roared and the glorious empire was shaken to its foundations by her refusal."[20]

Let's get this straight. The king was such a disgraceful husband that his queen publicly humiliated and disrespected him. "What are we going to do if the word gets out? Women and wives everywhere will be out of control!" The great Mecumen stepped forward with the solution. Out of fear that "the word might get out," these men quickly drafted a decree that *got the word out* across the entire empire! Furthermore, this was to be done in an effort to control, potential, out of control wives. The men were foolish indeed! Rather than addressing and controlling their own hearts and lack of character, they decided to make a decree to control others. Rather than changing and being husbands worthy of respect, they decided to demand respect. While I hope you are seeing the humorous irony of these moments, we must also be careful. Before we look down our pharisaical noses at these guys and their foolish decree, we would do well to humbly recognize the foolish decrees that our own hearts have made and continue to make.

Actually, "God, where are you," is not so much a genuine, humble inquiry of God's whereabouts. It is often a demand, spoken in disgust. It is a decree from my deceitful heart. At that moment, when the "God, where are you" decree is spoken, I know God is sovereign and that is why, through clenched teeth, I have spoken those words. I am decreeing some things, foolish things that are wrapped up in that moment as I assault the character of God.

---

[20] Iain M. Duguid. Esther & Ruth (Reformed Expository Commentary) (Kindle Locations 165-166). Kindle Edition.

God, you don't understand my suffering and what's more, you don't care what I am going through. I have prayed and prayed, and yet I only grow increasingly sick.... God, where are you? Let's be honest with our hearts. You and I are not beyond king Ahasuerus moments. We too buy into the foolish counsel that is in us or surrounds us. We buy into it because it's what we want to hear. By God's grace, I have had the joy of repenting of my foolish decrees over the years. It is at this point I join with Paul in Romans 7 as the apostle has been wrestling with his sinful flesh when he asks:

Wretched man that I am! Who will deliver me from this body of death? Thanks be to God through Jesus Christ our Lord!

Romans 7:24-25

Yes, we too have sipped the kool-aid of foolish counselors. Let's keep digging a little deeper and think about these guys who were given the incredible task to bring counsel to the king. How were these men, who desired favor and all that the king could offer, going to be able to stand up to the king? Will they counsel the most powerful man in the world with what he *wants* to hear or will they offer him what he *needs* to hear?

What the king needs to hear is, "oh great king, you're being arrogant, self-centered, and frankly, you're being a jerk. Humble yourself and ask the queen to forgive you!" Hopefully, they would say it with more gentleness and wisdom but that is the summary of what the king needs to hear. In their lust for power and position, the counselors will opt to stroke his ego and kiss his ring.

And so, the advisors feed the pride, self-centeredness, and self-preservation of the king. Let us consider: what kind of counselors have we gathered around us? I have heard individuals say: "I don't do the counseling thing." But what is "the counseling thing?" Initially, it doesn't sound like something I want to do either! Friends, all of us have counselors and all of us give counsel. It may not be *professional*, paid counseling that takes place behind a desk, as if a desk and a diploma suddenly make for good counsel. No, it is likely over the phone, through a text, or at the cafe´. It might be brief, perhaps long. Spontaneous or planned, *all* of us give and receive counsel. The question is not *if* we are giving and receiving counsel. The question is: *is the counsel we are giving and receiving any good?* Is it biblical, based in the truth and grace found in God's Word? Or is it anything more than the counsel the king received? Is it sympathy, telling us what we want to hear and confirming what we are already inclined to do? Or does it wisely and gently help us to see what we need to see? These men were token counselors.

The God Who Is There

It is amazing to see how God will use these fearful counselors to bring about His redemptive plan. Due to their counsel, the king decreed one thing and immediately turned and decreed another. Behold your gods. They are fickle, always changing to suit their whims. Where is God? He is the King who has decreed salvation and His Word is unchanging. In the midst of fallen man, God will have a people. He is orchestrating events to the working out of His redemption plan. Where is God in this text and where is God in our lives? When king Disease, king Cancer, or king Ahasuerus is speaking and decreeing from their throne, God is there! We can see the rulership of disease, failing relationships, or wayward children, and in those moments it can be terribly difficult to see God. We can hear these kings decree and yet our King seems strangely silent. What are we to do, how are we to think?

God IS At Work!

We struggle to see this in our own lives. That is why we have this little book, Esther. Watch it unfold as God orchestrates the sovereign deliverance of His people. We will soon see God's hand of rescue, sparing the people of Israel from genocide. Esther and Mordecai will emerge and become God's instruments of redemption to His people.

Why did Vashti refuse that simple command? Why did king Ahasuerus, who was probably under the influence of alcohol, make his foolish demand? Who came up with the idea of deposing Queen Vashti and replacing her with a better woman? Who will be the next queen and how will she be chosen by the king?

What about your life story? What about your seasons of suffering? Where is God in the pages of your life? Does it seem like your prayers continue to go unanswered? His seeming absence in no way indicates that He is not there. Though there are times that we cannot see God's activity in our lives, Esther exists to show us He is still sovereign. In the silence, God was altering history and redeeming lives!

Maybe some of us are experiencing a season where we have children who are wayward in their faith. Perhaps there are husbands that are not leading, caring, or serving at home. Or maybe there are wives who are distant and unloving. Have you been applying for a job and the doors always seem to slam shut? Or maybe you recently received a phone call from your doctor. Are you more familiar than you care to be with singleness with no prospects in sight?

Some of these are godly ambitions and desires but they have not come to fruition and you're wondering *God, where are you?* Take heart: God has promised to never leave us nor forsake us. Before there was the joy of the resurrection, there was the pain and suffering of the cross. In your suffering, He is there quietly working and bringing about His good purpose in our lives. Wait and trust in the able arms of the Lord. Your story has not ended; God is at work.

Esther Points Us To Jesus

King Ahasuerus' kingdom and his fallen ways lead us to another King and another Kingdom! The book of Esther is a big street sign that points us to the one true King. God the Father also has laws and He too has issued decrees that will not be revoked! However, there is quite a difference between these two kings, their decrees, and their responses to law-breakers. While king Ahasuerus' laws were written for his personal gain, God's laws were written for our benefit. King Ahasuerus desired to use Queen Vashti for his glory and selfish purpose. He then banished the law-breaker from his presence thus destroying their relationship. We too have dissed the King and dismissed His decrees. But our loving King has not banished us from His presence. No, the King sent His Son to make a way for us to be brought into a restored relationship with Him. He has made a way for the law-breaker to repent and to be made right. Indeed, rather than banishing decree breakers, the King adopts the wayward law breakers and makes us His children!

King Ahasuerus threw an opulent feast complete with curtains, fine linens, marble pillars, extravagant couches, and golden vessels filled with the royal wine. Our Lord and King has also prepared a banquet for us. However, when He calls us to His banquet, He does not throw a big party for the important "somebodies" among us. On the contrary, He invites the outcasts and the foreigners! He invites me and you, the commoners, to sit at His banquet table! And when we gather on that future day, He will not expose us to our shame in the midst of drunkenness. He will lavish His blessings upon us; He will expose us to His grace and mercy. He will look upon us as His beloved children and not mere objects of His possession.[21]

It is easy to see why Vashti refused the king's command to be paraded in front of foul-smelling, drunken men. But that's not the kind of invitation that we have from our King. The King is our Father who wants us to experience His full blessings. The King is Jesus, His Son, who laid down His life for our sins.

King Ahasuerus was a lousy husband; his relationship with the queen, at best, was impersonal. If she approached the king without being summoned, her punishment was potential death. Ahasuerus was preoccupied with amassing power, property, control, and riches. He was self-centered and self-absorbed; on the contrary, Christ emptied Himself.[22] King Ahasuerus treated Vashti disrespectfully, our King is the groom who loves us unconditionally, sacrificially and graciously.[23] Whereas, king Ahasuerus was consumed with beautiful women, King Jesus died for the unattractive and the unlovely. He did not seek to be served but to serve and give

---

[21] Iain M. Duguid. Esther & Ruth (Reformed Expository Commentary) (Kindle Locations 238-241). Kindle Edition.

[22] Philippians 2:7

[23] Ephesians 5:25-32

41

up His life as a ransom for many.[24] Jesus Christ died for the ungodly,[25] while we were still sinners,[26] his enemies.[27]

Behold your God, behold your King! For our sake He made Him to be sin who knew no sin so that in Him we might become the righteousness of Christ.[28] With this kind of love, why wouldn't we come to Him when He calls us? The gracious call of the King becomes irresistible!

Who, then, does our allegiance belong to? Do we offer our loyalty to an earthly kingdom of glitz, glamor and false happiness that will one day pass away? If you have found yourself placing your allegiance to such things, then I encourage you to flee from these false gods and run to the One who is the everlasting, gracious King.

King Ahasuerus seemingly had everything and yet he had nothing. He had the appearance of being in control. All the while, everything was spinning out of his control. *The* King, while never named, was sovereignly ruling and reigning accomplishing His master plan of salvation! To read Esther is to behold the glory of our redemption. What great depths has the Lord gone to accomplish your salvation? How sovereign has He been over the details of your life? God, where are you? Behold your God!

Reflections:

- Does your life seem like it's spinning out of control while God is seemingly silent in it all?

- If so, what Scriptures do you need to memorize and meditate on to root yourself in the truths of God's sovereignty?

---

[24] Mark 10:45

[25] Romans 5:6

[26] Romans 5:8

[27] Romans 5:10

[28] 2 Corinthians 5:21

Chapter 4: **When Kingdoms Collide**

"I'm fairly convinced that the Kingdom of God is for the broken-hearted. You write of 'powerlessness.' Join the club, we are not in control. God is. "

Fred Rogers

Ours is a culture that, by in large, views God's Word as irrelevant. After all, what does a culture of beauty contests, the threat of death to an entire race, anger, power, authority, risk, drunkenness, and lavish displays of wealth found in the book of Esther have to do with us living in the 21st century? How are we to look at this ancient book? How are we to relate to a culture that placed an inordinate amount of value on the wealth of a man or the beauty of a woman? The ancient magazine racks at the Persian market would have looked similar to ours today!

As we explore the details of the book of Esther we will find that while styles have changed, the human condition remains the same throughout the ages and kingdoms continue to collide then and now. My goal in this chapter is to help us see just how relevant God's Word is to our lives. But first, we need to take a brief look at Persian History 101.

The king's History

Our little history lesson is important as it will help us gain insight into the making of the man, king Ahasuerus.

The downward spiral of God's Old Testament people repeats like a bad scratch on an old vinyl record. God's people, continually turned their backs against Him to worship false gods. Therefore, God raised up pagan nations to bring judgment and turn their hearts back to Him. Remember Cyrus from Chapter one? He was the Persian king who unseated the Babylonians and released the captive Israelites. King Cyrus' reign came to an abrupt end when he was killed on the battlefield. Eventually, Darius became king of the vast Persian empire. Under king Darius, the Persians desired to vanquish the Greeks due to their participation in the Ionian Revolt. This uprising sought to unseat the Persian rule in the city of Ionia. The Persians crushed the revolt and subsequently invaded the Greeks in Marathon. The Greeks were vastly overpowered and outnumbered by the Persians. Due to this advantage, the Persians sought to deliver a death blow to their enemy. However, Darius' army was out maneuvered and soundly defeated by Miltiades.[29]

The Persians' long march home was marked with shame. Their defeat was unimaginable. How could such a powerful force be defeated by the lesser Greek army? On the one hand, the Battle of Marathon became a pivotal moment in the rise of the Greeks, as they were emboldened by their improbable victory. On the other hand, the once invincible Persian army had been exposed. Enraged and humiliated, king Darius was determined to rebuild his colossal army and lead it to victory. As providence would have it, Darius died before leading the revenge. The baton was then passed to his son Xerxes / Ahasuerus. Xerxes was driven to restore the honor of his father![30]

In order to move his massive army, Ahasuerus had to build bridges across the Hellespont. The Hellespont was a narrow strip of water between the Aegean Sea and the Sea of Marmara. The work was completed when the Persian army began its march across the newly built bridges. The smell of victory was in the air when a violent storm emerged and destroyed the bridges. Ahasuerus was furious with both the storm and the bridge's engineers. In a child-like fit of rage, the king had his engineers' heads chopped off. He also sent his well-trained warriors, armed with whips, into the sea to

---

[29] The battle of Marathon inspired what we now know as the marathon race. The legend states that the Greek messenger Pheidippides ran 26 miles to Athens exclaiming the surprise news of Greek victory.

[30] http://www.perseus.tufts.edu/hopper/text?doc=Perseus%3Atext%3A1999.01.0126&redirect=true

deliver 300 lashes upon the water. Now appropriately punished, the sea permitted the Persians to cross. However, the vast army arrived late to the battle and, once again, the outnumbered Greeks defeated the massive Persian army! Consequently, humiliation and devastation fell upon the Persians. Eventually, Alexander the Great rose to power and led the Greeks into ultimate victory by soundly defeating the Persians.[31]

Many of those Greco-Persians battles were led by Ahasuerus and some speculate that these skirmishes took place between Esther 1 and 2. Badly defeated and disgraced, we might imagine this powerful king under the weight of a severe depression.[32]

Relevant Regret

We have all sipped that bitter taste of regret. Words spoken, acts committed, and thoughts unsaid are all included in the abyss of regret. *What was I thinking, why did I say that, where did those wicked thoughts come from?* Esther 2 begins with the mighty king wallowing in deep regret.

*After these things, when the anger of King Ahasuerus had abated, he **remembered** Vashti and what she had done and what had been decreed...*

Esther 2:1

The party was over and the queen was gone, having been banished foolishly. Now sobered, the king "remembered Vashti." Our English translation of the word "remember" doesn't fully capture the weight of that moment. Bryan Gregory helps us when he writes;

> *The word translated "remember" means much more than simply recalling to mind the pertinent information; it has a more robust sense to it, having the connotation of recalling something with affection, almost like nostalgia. In other words, Ahasuerus is*

---

[31] https://www.gty.org/library/sermons-library/80-392/esther-for-such-a-time-as-this

[32] http://www.history.com/topics/ancient-history/battle-of-marathon

not simply reviewing dispassionately the events that have transpired; he remembers Vashti warmly and is stricken with regret over the way he treated her. Perhaps he is sorry for his initial summons. Perhaps he is sorry that she complicated the matter by not coming when summoned. Perhaps he is sorry that he acted so rashly. Or perhaps he realizes what he has lost, now that she is gone, and he misses her. Whatever the reasons for his regret, however, there is nothing he can do about it now. He acted impetuously, and now she is irretrievably gone.[33]

It is possible that the king had come to a place of regret for his foolish decree against Vashti. Was he lonely and depressed? While we don't know all that the king might have been remembering, we are more familiar than we care to be with our own "remembering." We might remember our own foolish actions in a moment of anger. Many undesired divorces have resulted from spiteful words spoken out of bitterness. Vows abandoned, promises unfulfilled as married couples do the unthinkable. No couple stood at the altar dreaming of this day. Regrets abound! But marriage doesn't have a monopoly on regret. Regret is the reminder of the foolishness of sin, married or single.

As believers rooted in all that Christ has accomplished on the cross, we have the joy of chasing our memories of regretful thoughts by remembering Christ's sacrifice. Ultimately, your memory of the mountain of past sins is no match for Calvary's hill! Christ's once-for-all sacrifice delivered a death blow to that mountain of regret. Some say, "if you only knew all that I have done." But friend, if you only knew all that Christ has accomplished!

Isn't that *part* of the purpose of the Lord's Supper? Jesus calls on us to remember his body and his blood as often as we eat the bread or drink of the cup.[34] Regret is relevant. That is why we must look to Jesus!

---

[33] Gregory, Bryan R. (2014-12-30). Inconspicuous Providence: The Gospel According to Esther (Gospel According to the Old Testament) P&R Publishing.

[34] I Corinthians 11:24-25

...the founder and perfecter of our faith, who for the joy that was set before him endured the cross, despising the shame, and is seated at the right hand of the throne of God.

Hebrews 12:2

Relevant Counseling

Apparently, the "young men who attended to Ahasuerus" realized something was wrong with their king (2:1-4). These men gathered to strategize how they might put their powerful king back together again. Their suggested strategy shed light on the king's regret. "Round up all the young, beautiful, virgin women." Are you not amazed at the relevance of God's Word in our lives? We can imagine the depressed king. His army was crushed by the inferior Greeks, the queen was long gone, and so the advisors drafted up a plan to cheer up their king.

It is in these life moments of feeling deflated that our next move is critical. When the memories come flooding in, we need the counsel of God's Word "a lamp to my feet, a light to my path."[35] Now, Ahasuerus was a king who thought of himself as a god, so we should not expect him to turn to God for wisdom. Although, what about us? Is it reasonable that in our moments of regret, despair, and loneliness we would turn to God for counsel and wisdom? Sadly, far too often Christians prefer to commiserate in their misery. Wisdom provided by God Himself goes unsearched; the Word of the living God remains on the shelf. Prayerless saints and Wordless Christians search for answers in a thousand *other* places.

It would be odd for the king to turn to godly counsel, though it's not unimaginable. Improbable, maybe, but not impossible. Pharaoh was more than willing to pursue Joseph for the interpretation of his dreams.[36] Daniel, Nehemiah, and others were used by God to bring counsel to pagan kings. But, not this king, not this kingdom. Rather than humbly pursuing wise counsel that seeks to speak the truth, he turned to his puppet advisors. As we have previously seen,

---

[35] Psalm 119:105

[36] See Genesis 41

these advisors tell us what we want to hear so that we feel free to go do what we have already determined to do. We are not looking for truth. We do not want to be counseled; we want to be agreed with and justified in our opinions. We know the sort, as we too have our puppet advisors.

While the marriage is crashing, the husband searches for a voice who will take his side and find agreement with his headstrong opinions. He thinks "after all, I am right." She is on a similar pursuit as she seeks to find that person who will stand up to her husband and tell him what he needs to hear. She too thinks "after all, I am right." Neither one is looking for counsel; both are looking for agreement.

At the counseling appointment, the husband and wife defend their respective sides. It's easy to walk through the right motions and remain unwilling to apply God's Word to our hearts. He sits aghast that his faults would be pointed out. She is shocked that the counselor has not taken her side. I wonder: *why do they go through the effort?* I imagine the next conversation he shares with a close friend: "we tried the counseling thing, it didn't work for us." In other words: *the counselor didn't see it my way; he agreed with her and attacked me. I would never go back and sit through that again.* Now, I am not beyond this one-sided mindset. I too have pursued counsel that agrees with my *infallible* perception of things. Caution: your next move is crucial and it has the potential to make a miserable situation fall deeper into the abyss!

It is here that we must see the foolishness of the counsel the king received. "Your life is falling apart, oh king, get yourself a beautiful woman. Yes, that is what you need. Eye-candy will fix everything for you!" Are these guys serious? This world has no shortage of these counselors and these kinds of shallow answers. Life is falling apart. You are miserable and the counselors around you advise you to: have an affair, find a new relationship, divorce your spouse, find a new husband or wife. Still not happy? Drink away your sorrows, eat a bag of potato chips, buy a car, amass debt, go on a spontaneous vacation. A litany of other foolish counsel is offered that only brings grief in the end. Recognize when the friend at the water cooler says; "you don't need that ball and chain" or "you deserve to get out and live it up," you have been counseled foolishly.

Sadly, many marriages and families have reaped the destruction created right there in those water cooler moments. If you are one of those who have walked this bitter road of regret and has come to a place of repentance, then you know of God's forgiveness and relational restoration. But, for those of you who are tempted to listen to the foolish counsel found on every street corner of your life, Esther is relevant!

Counseling that is worth your time is going to be difficult. Good counsel is difficult counsel. I have benefited from that good, difficult counsel many times. We might not enjoy it when a friend holds up the mirror of God's Word and exposes our hearts, but it is good! Sadly, sometimes we would rather continue on our self-deception and destructive thinking. In the name of self-preservation, we destroy ourselves and others. We, like Adam, prefer to camouflage ourselves in the bushes seeking to hide from God. We are afraid of exposure to the light of God's Word. We do not want to be known and this desire is to our great detriment. I encourage you, where needed, humble yourself and find a friend who will speak the truth in love.[37] If you are receiving counsel that is rooted in pleasing you, the king, then run! Why pursue that counsel that says "go with your lust filled desires and ignore God's wisdom?"

This pleased the king, and he did so.

Esther 2:4

These counselors knew how to appease the king: advise him to do what will bring him pleasure. The sinfulness of man has not changed in the past 2000+ years. What the king needed, and our hearts need, is to dethrone the king of me and seek the One who is seated on His throne, King Jesus! The king's hope and our hope will not be found in a simple fix of false saviors. What our hearts need is something much more profound. We need Christ and the glories of His grace applied to our hearts!

---

[37] Ephesians 4:15

The Relevant Beauty Contest

Have you ever tried to lose a contest? Perhaps while playing a game of HORSE with your 10-year-old son or chess with your 8-year-old daughter. Well, as you read the advice of the king's men, imagine you are a young lady living in Susa. Ladies, this was a contest you didn't want to win! Hide your beauty and scheme up a way to go unnoticed. The winner of the king's beauty contest will become the king's property. Oh boy…!

There are only three requirements for the potential new queen: beauty, youth, and virginity. These are the values that made the list back in ancient days. Imagine the horror of having your daughter, sister, or the woman you hoped to marry snatched from your sight, carted off to be placed into the royal harem. The custom of the day left no options. When your daughter or sister was called upon, you were to be compliant. In a moment's notice, she was snatched and you would likely never see her again. This act was legalized sex trafficking practiced by the government for the all-powerful king. The young and beautiful were powerless to resist. If you are the not-so-lucky winner of this contest, you were expected to marry the man who had divorced his previous bride in a drunken rage. Additionally, if you were not chosen to be the queen, you were not sent home. You lived out your days in the royal harem, never to marry, never to have children; a mere object among the rest of the king's possessions. While the woman's character was not a consideration, the king's character has been on display. He was a dominating, self-absorbed husband that had shown no care for his former wife or for women in general. He was arrogant and easily angered, happy to round up women for himself. A powerful man gone wrong, a king without a conscience.

So, line up ladies! Who wants to be a millionaire? We all know that beauty is skin deep. Physical beauty is fleeting. It's just a matter of time before the ladies who were chosen based on their appearances will no longer have the necessary beauty. Ladies, if you build your entire life around your beauty, eventually that life will fail you. Oh, the folly of the world we live in today! As people question the relevance of the Bible in our day, our culture has created beauty contests played out weekly on reality tv shows. Pull up a chair; it is tantalizing entertainment. Let's not distance ourselves from "those" people on the screen. Our hearts are also drawn to the folly found within the pages of Esther.

Relevant Kingdoms Collide

*Now there was a Jew in Susa the citadel whose name was Mordecai, the son of Jair, son of Shimei, son of Kish, a Benjaminite, who had been **carried away** from Jerusalem among the captives **carried away** with Jeconiah king of Judah, whom Nebuchadnezzar king of Babylon had **carried away**.*

Esther 2:5-6

The writer of Esther tells us that Mordecai lived in Susa because the Jews had been "carried away from Jerusalem." Furthermore, we are given a brief lineage of Mordecai. Consider the diamond in these details. Why does the author of Esther tell us, three times, that the descendants of Saul were "carried away." We are to read both of these pieces and think: *something is not right here!*

Remember, Cyrus had released the Jews and provided them an opportunity to return to Jerusalem. And, if you were a Jew living in Susa, you should do just that. Return to your home and live among the worshiping community of God. It is in your blood, Mordecai! Your descendants were carried away and you are a part of the direct lineage of king Saul. These details show us that kingdoms are colliding.

Mordecai opted to remain in Susa which left Esther to be drawn into the king's lustful beauty contest, where she will spend a "night with the king." I want to shout at the written page, "Mordecai, run! Susa is not your home and Ahasuerus is not your king!" Hence, the author of Esther provides us with more evidence that things are not as they ought to be.

He was bringing up Hadassah, that is Esther, the daughter of his uncle, for she had neither father nor mother. The young woman had a beautiful figure and was lovely to look at, and when her father and her mother died, Mordecai took her as his own daughter. So when the king's order and his edict were proclaimed, and when many young women were gathered in Susa the citadel in custody of Hegai, Esther also was taken into the king's palace and put in custody of Hegai ...

Esther 2:7-8

We are told that Mordecai "....was bringing up Hadassah." Hadassah was Esther's Hebrew name. Did you know that? I always thought of Esther as...well...Esther. I have never referred to her as Hadassah. And, though I have read the story many times, this bit of information has always eluded me. Esther was Hadassah's *Persian* (or pagan) name. It was not the name given to her at birth, rather, it was the name given to her to blend into Persian culture.[38] What is the point? The two names are mentioned here to be yet another reminder that kingdoms are colliding. The author is telling us that they were Jews, *carried away* far from home with a family tree linked to Israel's first king, complete with a Persian name! All of this data is written to clue us in that they belong to another Kingdom under another King.

As Mordecai lingered in the pagan city of this world, I find it helpful to read Esther 2 as if I don't know the rest of the story. Doing so causes me to be stirred to shout at our friend and yell at myself, "Mordecai, get out of Susa, and....Tim, run from this world, you two don't belong there!" God's Word tells us in Romans that we are not to be conformed to this world, but we are to be transformed...[39] We are strangers in this world, just passing through to our eternal home with Christ.[40] While we live in the world, we are not of this world.[41] Our citizenship is in heaven, and from it we await a Savior, the Lord Jesus Christ."[42]

Instead, it seems Mordecai and Esther are *in* the world and *of* the world. Rather than transforming their world, the world was

---

[38] Crossway Bibles (2009-04-09). ESV Study Bible (Kindle Locations 59707-59710). Good News Publishers/Crossway Books. Kindle Edition.

[39] Romans 12:2

[40] I Peter 2:11

[41] John 17:14-15

[42] Philippians 3:20

transforming them. Friends, our Susa wants your conformity! It lures us to put down roots and live this life as if it's all we've got. It tempts us to dismiss our Christian identity. We live in two colliding kingdoms. We like our comforts here in our Susa and we desire to enjoy the benefits of the Kingdom of God.

And the young woman pleased him and won his favor. And he quickly provided her with her cosmetics and her portion of food.... **Esther had not made known her people or kindred, for Mordecai had commanded her not to make it known.** *(This command by Mordecai is repeated in verse 20.)*

Esther 2:9-10

Esther was now in a position of compromise and danger. So much so, that Mordecai instructed Esther *not to make known* her people. In essence, Mordecai was saying, "Esther, do not reveal that you belong to the people of God! You are a Jew but don't act like one. Don't use your Jewish name, suppress your Jewish identity, and blend into the kingdom." We need to realize the extent of this denial of her Jewish identity. Persian dress, Persian customs, and Persian society were all a part of who she had become. Clearly, she blended in enough to the Persian world to fool the king. She counted the cost, rolled the dice, and lived a Persian life. This decision led to compromises regarding Sabbath keeping, sexual immorality, marrying someone of a foreign nation, and much more.[43]

Conceal your identity and blend into the culture. This is the temptation when kingdoms collide. Sadly, we too are enticed to do exactly what Mordecai suggested to Esther. Indeed, when my comfort and love of this world exceeds my desire for honoring God, suppressing who I am in Christ often quickly follows. Hard work awaits them back in Jerusalem and hard work awaits us as we seek to follow Christ. It is much easier to live for the world than to live for Christ. Like Mordecai, we might not be outright denying God but we too are tempted to take the path of least resistance. Pursuing whatever sin that presents itself, as long as it suits us, is effortless. Following Christ, however, is a daily dying to self.

---

[43] This theme is further developed by Tim Keller in his series on Esther. http://www.gospelinlife.com/esther-and-the-hiddenness-of-god

Sadly, many of us want to have our King and our king. Susa is enticing and following Jesus can be difficult. At the same time, we know that He is truth and eternity with Him awaits us. Conformity calls us to keep enough of Jesus in our pockets so that, when we need Him, we can pull Him out and call on Him. Sadly, Jesus becomes little more than a Genie in a bottle. When needed rub the lamp and, poof - God appears to grant you your wish. Be warned, loving this world and suppressing who you are in Christ is a dangerous affair.

Sure, Esther gained much worldly success, but at what expense? She married and became queen to the most powerful king in the world. But she did so at a great cost. Yes, kingdoms collided in those ancient days and they still collide today. What is the follower of Christ to do? Christians are killed, imprisoned, and tortured throughout the world today because they refuse to deny Christ. Those realities seem distant to those of us who are living in the West, surrounded and consumed by the comforts of our Susa. I am afraid, in the West, we think too little of Jesus' words to *deny yourself and take up your cross and follow me...* Some assume this means we might be disliked a little by friends and family. Or perhaps it means that we will be ridiculed a bit behind our backs by co-workers at the office. Maybe it means we are to suffer by waking up early and going to that prayer meeting that was announced at church last Sunday. Wherever you call home, kingdoms collide daily. Will we serve the kings of this world that play to our comforts? Will we silence who we are in Christ? Or will we live for King Jesus who has "called us out of the darkness and into his light?"[44] John Piper calls this a *"sacred schizophrenia."* He writes:

> *When you hear yourself say: "I don't want opposition; I want approval. I don't want shame; I want honor. I don't want suffering; I want comfort and the pleasures of this world. I don't want to die; I want to be safe and secure and to stay alive. So, no! I will not take up my cross" - when you hear yourself say that, you - your other self - must say, "You are no longer in charge! I deny you the right to hold any sway in this matter. So you be quiet. You are not my true self anymore. You*

---

[44] I Peter 2:9

are passing away. Your days are numbered. It is I and not you who will live forever. So keep your desires to yourself.[45]

How relevant is this kingdom? In the kingdom of man, you too can be handpicked by the king. We all want to be liked and accepted; none of us desires rejection from the higher ups of this world. There is a little pattern one can invoke to win the prize of worldly acceptance. I wonder if we might recognize this pattern in our own lives.

First, if we want to climb the ranks in the kingdom of this world, we must begin by covering up our identity as a child of God. Like Esther, we must heed Mordecai's instruction and begin to blend into the kingdom. The imperative becomes: follow the rules and play the empires games. When we choose the comforts of this world over the pursuit of God, man pleasing soon follows. As the morality of our world declines, our resolve to follow God, and not man, must increase.

...am I now seeking the approval of man, or of God? Or am I trying to please man? If I were still trying to please man, I would not be a servant of Christ.

Galatians 1:10

"The fear of man lays a snare, but whoever trusts in the Lord is safe."

Proverbs 29:25

We should note that Daniel took a very different approach than Mordecai and Esther. When kingdoms collided, Daniel refused to fear the king, instead, he feared *the* King (Daniel 3). Second, appearances are everything. Having been chosen, the ladies were given twelve months for "beautifying" (Esther 2:12). Wow, twelve months! As we consider this scene, once again, we are confronted with how little things have changed. If you are a man, wealth and power will get you somewhere. And, if you are a woman, appearances

---

[45] http://www.desiringgod.org/messages/sacred-schizophrenia

are the ticket for your advancement in the kingdoms of this world. The whole book of Esther seems to be driven by appearances. The kingdom came crashing down due to one beautiful woman and was then rebuilt because of another. It is a superficial kingdom that regards external beauty above the inner beauty of the heart. The Kingdom of God points us away from the fleeting folly of outward appearances. *But the LORD said to Samuel, "Do not look on his appearance or on the height of his stature, because I have rejected him. For the LORD sees not as man sees: man looks on the outward appearance, but the LORD looks on the heart." I Samuel 16:7*

Peter, speaking of external beauty says *"...Let your adorning be the hidden person of the heart with the imperishable beauty of a gentle and quiet spirit, which in God's sight is very precious."*[46] Beauty, not character, is what the king desired. I ask as you consider our day, a few thousand years later, has anything changed? Is our world driven by character or beauty? What gains recognition, power, position, and wealth?

A message to young ladies: Please, do not buy into the lie of our culture. Ours is a day that looks much like the pages of this ancient book. It saddens me to see what a young lady will do to win the "king's" contest. Ladies, "do not be conformed to this world, but be transformed."[47]

A message to young men: Do not create this contest in your own heart. If beauty is the god you desire, it is only a matter of time before your god will fail you. If you marry for physical beauty alone, you are placing an enormous pressure on your wife. However, if your definition of beauty is built on that "imperishable beauty" that Peter spoke of, you will avoid needless temptations and manipulations.

---

[46] I Peter 3:4

[47] Romans 12:2

...when the young woman went in to the king in this way, she was given whatever she desired to take with her from the harem to the king's palace. In the evening she would go in, and in the morning she would return to the second harem.... She would not go in to the king again, unless the king delighted in her and she was summoned by name.

Esther 2:13

Esther was a compliant child of the empire. We might even say she was anti-Vashti.[48] To be sure, that is what brought her worldly success. After all, she did become the queen which then positioned her to be offered much by her king.

Now, I know what you are thinking. "But, if she didn't obey, then she wouldn't have become the queen. And, if she didn't become queen, then she wouldn't have been able to appeal to the king and the Jews wouldn't have been saved." To that, I ask: "How big is your God?" Amazingly, Esther's conformity did not write her out of the story. Behold the mercy of our God! Yet, if God is able to save His people from destruction through the means of her disobedience, then it is safe to assume that God could have saved his people through her obedience.

The glory of the story is not that God *needed* Esther to become queen to later save His people. The glory of Esther is that God moved "for such a time as this..." *in spite of* Esther and Mordecai. The glory is not Esther's work; it is God's work through Esther. Likewise, the glory of our story is not that God needs us; it is that God saves and uses us in spite us!

Reflections:

- How might you be suppressing your identity to win the approval of the king in our Susa?

- In what ways has the kingdoms of this world and the Kingdom of God collided in your everyday life?

---

[48] This term comes from Iain M. Duguid. Esther & Ruth (Reformed Expository Commentary) (Kindle Location 347). Kindle Edition.

Chapter 5: Two Kingdoms, Two Gospels

"When I think of how I came to saving faith, there is no denying God's involvement. I was born in the Philippines into a wealthy family. My dad was a successful owner of several stores. We had a big house complete with servants and nannies who lived down stairs. Then, unthinkable hard times came in a season of suffering. My dad became very sick and eventually, he died. The business went into decline and eventually we lost all the stores! The wealth we once knew soon disappeared due to medical bills and the lack of income. My mom was a 42-year-old widow seeking to provide for her six young children. We had no money; I remember being regularly hungry! She began to participate in a pen pal program where she would write to a man named Charles Bowman. He too was a widower who had recently retired as a successful mechanic with the Chicago Transit Authority. All six of his daughters were grown. He could have easily retired and enjoyed the benefits of his hard work. What were the odds that this man would one day meet and marry my mother? Amazingly, that is exactly what happened. Charles Bowman married my mom and lived with us in the Philippines until they felt that a move was in our best interest. In 1980, we all moved to the United States and it is here that my Sunday school teacher shared the Gospel with me. She had a heart for us kids. I met my Savior at around the age of ten in that Sunday school. Now, do you think all these circumstances were coincidences? By no means! God was at work in all the details. He orchestrated every event at the right place, and the right time, because he was redeeming. In hindsight, the hand of God was all over that season of my life. He was at work before I knew Him, working out my salvation for my good and for His glory!"

Alex Bowman

Now Esther was winning favor in the eyes of all who saw her. And when Esther was taken to King Ahasuerus, into his royal palace, in the tenth month, which is the month of Tebeth, in the seventh year of his reign, the king loved Esther more than all the women, and she won grace and favor in his sight more than all the virgins, so that he set the royal crown on her head and made her queen instead of Vashti. Then the king gave a great feast for all his officials and servants; it was Esther's feast.

Esther 2:15-18

The Gospel According To The Kingdoms Of This World

Kingdoms continue to collide as there are opposing kingdom gospels. The Gospel means good news and this world offers us good news of many sorts. All we need to do is to count the cost, comply with the culture, conform to its values, and this world's so-called good news can be ours. The saviors of this world include wealth, acceptance, a comfortable lifestyle, education, and relationships just to name a few. We are tutored by our culture to believe in this deceptive gospel. This *good news* defines for us the happy life, the life you wish you had, the life of gratification. And yet, it still rains on the "just and the unjust."[49] Stock markets continue to crash and floods do not deviate their way around the houses of the rich and famous. Thus far, even the wealthiest have yet to find a way to dodge chronic illness. This is what makes the good news of Jesus Christ good news. The true Gospel offers us a salvation beyond a nicer car or a bigger house with a white picket fence.

Powerball mania happens once or twice a year. It always amazes me to see complete strangers joyfully chatting like long-lost friends about the possibility of holding the winning ticket. The Powerball is a type of savior that offers hope to lift you from the pit to the apex of a problem-free life. In spite of the many articles written about the destroyed lives that many winners experience, we want in!

---

[49] Matthew 5:45

We dream of a better life that rises above life's challenges. The winners of the 2016 Powerball won the $1.58 billion prize! They live in my neighboring town of Melbourne Beach, Florida. I have often wondered how it turned out for them. Has the gospel of wealth delivered them from the stress of this world?

Many relationships have been wrecked by this world's false gospels. Brenda is a Christian who compromised her convictions to marry her knight in shining armor. He was not a Christian but she was convinced that he was "such a good guy." She couldn't imagine her life without him. The wedding was stunning but the marriage was built on false hopes. Now that they are "until death do us part," she finds he is not the savior she once dreamed. Distant from God and crying herself to sleep, she wonders, *what happened?*

John is a young man who went to an Ivy League school which assured him a fast track to a six-figure salary. This good news gospel promised a career field that would amount to a life of constant pleasure. He always wanted to travel the world and this career vowed to give him that opportunity. But the University's website did not have a tab explaining the mountain of debt and the lack of job prospects upon graduation. His gospel of success left him depressed, as he now works long hours at the local coffee shop seeking to make ends meet.

John's college roommate, Steve, graduated and landed that dream job. He seemingly has it all. Vacations to ski resorts around the world and a garage filled with the finest cars. Sure, his work takes him away from his family but look at his success. Who wouldn't want that? Answer: Steve's wife, Kelly, and their three children! As they live this world's good news gospel, the family is miserable. Steve tries to buy his wife's happiness and yet the marriage continues to crumble. Disillusioned by his first gospel, he searches for another savior. He can now be found drinking late into the night, seeking to drown out the wreck he once called the dream life. He has become bitter and angry around the family. His mantra remains, "she refuses to see all that I have given to her." He starts to daydream about another woman at work who seems to truly appreciate what he can offer her in the way of travel and wealth. John shipwrecks his family to pursue yet another lie, another woman, another gospel.

Scott and Susan's marriage was headed for the cliff and they knew it. Only married for three years, they could not imagine remaining married for the rest of their lives. What happened? The gospel of marriage bliss led them to the altar; Susan carried a beautiful bouquet of flowers and a bag of lies. They thought they were to be the ultimate fulfillment of one another. That's what they told their pastor during premarital counseling. "Why do you want to get married?" Their reply came in gleeful unison: "because we complete each other - we are the perfect fit!" And so Scott and Susan dove into marriage with both feet. She didn't understand why he no longer showed her tender affection and he grew bitter over her snide comments. Rather than putting their trust and hope in the gospel of Jesus Christ, they determined to continue to chase other gospels. A new offer of hope became a part of the discussion. The good news of having a child would certainly be the jolt their marriage needed. Unsurprisingly, the joy of their newborn quickly became a source of new found anger. Once high school sweethearts, now they are little more than bitter roommates. She was beautiful in her wedding gown. However, after two children and inevitable aging, he is now drawn to other women. She feels the pressure to look just right but she can't compete with the magazine rack. Scott and Susan have both lost themselves in this world's false gospels.

Single, married, divorced, remarried or retired, we wreck our lives in a thousand ways upon the rocks that this world calls "the good life." We pursue these false, good news gospels that promise us a salvation from the strains of life. When we place our hope in them, though circumstances may change, our problems chase us. Friends excitedly comment on the shiny new car, new spouse, new home, new whatever, but the shine becomes dull when all else around us is failing. There is a hope that does not fade even when circumstances are not what we imagined.

Have you bought this world's bag of lies, this world's gospel? Is your hope wrapped up in the values of our culture? Is wealth or appearance the gospel that you believe will deliver you in the kingdom of this world? Our culture is not unlike Esther's. Beauty and sexual prowess are what brought Esther to power and wealth. I guess we could say Esther won the Powerball lottery. The book of Esther is an opportunity for us to peer in on Esther, the winner.

If you were living in the days of Esther, and if you were picked to be the queen of Persia, you would have likely received the favor of the king. From this point forward, life as you knew it would have been effortless. No more dirty laundry or washing the dishes! Such good news, you were instantly living the good life!

For what does it profit a man to gain the whole world and forfeit his soul? For what can a man give in return for his soul?

Mark 8:37

The favor that results from being accepted by the kings of this world comes at quite a cost. I wonder: *what was it like for Esther the first time she slipped on the queen's crown?* Standing before the mirror, did she have a sense that she had made it? Perhaps this was more appealing than I have previously described. Conceivably, all the young maidens longed to be the king's bride. A commoner like Esther lived a life of poverty without a shred of hope of anything changing. It is possible that being snatched from her home by the king's men was a promising moment in a young woman's life.

Esther became queen of the most powerful empire in the world! Wealth and a life of ease surrounded her. She had gone from being a lowly woman to having servants available at her beckoning. We read that she had servants dedicated to her beauty, and that was *before* she had become the queen!

However, these passing offers of good news fade like the morning dew. The Gospel of Jesus Christ remains the good news for sinners who have sabotaged our very own lives. Christ came to offer you and me true hope found only in Him. This hope is not found in being powerful, wealthy, or beautiful. It is found in Jesus Christ!

What Is The Gospel?

Some think that the gospel is solely "good news" or that "God is love." True enough, the word gospel means "good news" and God definitely is love but we need to ask: what is this "good news?" How does God reveal His love towards us? To answer these questions we now turn to the Gospel.

God Is Holy

God is holy and without sin. Christ came and lived a sin free life, perfectly obeying the Father. Imagine, no sin! Perfect in words, thoughts, and actions, fully submitted to the Father. He is holy and His holiness demands that we too are to be without sin and therein lies our great problem. For God to disregard sin is to disregard who He is, He *is* Holy.

Man Is Sinful

God, who is holy, created humanity. When we consider Adam and Eve in the garden, we realize something has gone terribly wrong. Lusting to be like God, Adam and Eve bought the serpents lie and determined to go their own way by rejecting God's command. The sinfulness of man and the holiness of God cannot commingle. Consider how Scripture views us in our sinfulness:

"None is righteous, no, not one; no one understands; no one seeks for God. All have turned aside; together they have become worthless; no one does good, not even one."

Romans 3:10-12

...for all have sinned and fall short of the glory of God,

Romans 3:23

For the wages of sin is death, but the free gift of God is eternal life in Christ Jesus our Lord.

Romans 6:23

Because man is sinful and God is holy, our sin has separated us from God. This discrepancy means we have a serious and eternal obstacle. Our problem of sin is great! Left to ourselves we are helpless and hopeless. God in His holy love desires a relationship with His creation. Equally important, God in His holiness can not allow sinfulness to go unaddressed. How does a holy and loving God,

63

whose perfect holiness demands justice for sin, restore our relationship with Him? It is here that we find God's holy love and holy justice poured out for us.

Jesus Paid For Our Sins

We are unable to save ourselves from our sins. We try in vain to live better lives by doing good deeds. We might attempt to live a reputable, moral, and pure life but if we are honest, we know that we fail miserably. Our New Year's resolutions to "do better" and to "try harder" quickly fade into oblivion. As we fail yet again, we throw up our hands and say, "why bother?" We further reason with ourselves: *I am doing good enough. After all, nobody's perfect.* The good news is that God the Father sent His Son who came, born of a virgin, lived a perfect life and died on the cross for our sins. He substituted Himself for us by suffering and dying in our place. He took our place on the cross and received the death that our sins deserved. It is here that the justice of God and the love of God meet. God's justice was satisfied in that Christ took our sins and paid our debt. Sin did not go unpunished. Christ was punished in our place! And the love of God was met in that, "God *so loved* the world that He gave His only Son..." The believer in Jesus Christ now receives the righteousness of Christ. Christ took our sins and gave us His righteousness.

Sinful Man Is Now Able To Be Reconciled To God!

When we place our faith in Christ, we can then be brought into a right relationship with the holy God. Because of the life, death, and resurrection of Christ, we are invited to repent of our sins and trust in God for the forgiveness of sins. Doing so restores our relationship with God by making us right or righteous before God. Our holy God and Father no longer views us in our sinfulness; He now looks at us through His son's righteousness. This aspect of the Gospel is called justification. We are justified by the atoning work of Jesus Christ alone! Our salvation, then, is not based on anything that we have done. Rather, it is based completely on our Savior's sacrifice. This is good news indeed![50]

---

[50] If you are not familiar with the Gospel, or would like to study these themes more thoroughly, I would recommend Greg Gilbert's book "What Is The Gospel?" and Ray Ortland's book "The Gospel"

And you were dead in the trespasses and sins in which you once walked, following the course of this world, following the prince of the power of the air, the spirit that is now at work in the sons of disobedience—among whom we all once lived in the passions of our flesh, carrying out the desires of the body and the mind, and were by nature children of wrath, like the rest of mankind. **But God,** *being rich in mercy, because of the great love with which he loved us, even when we were dead in our trespasses, made us alive together with Christ—by grace you have been saved—and raised us up with him and seated us with him in the heavenly places in Christ Jesus, so that in the coming ages he might show the immeasurable riches of his grace in kindness toward us in Christ Jesus.* ***For by grace you have been saved through faith. And this is not your own doing; it is the gift of God, not a result of works, so that no one may boast.*** *For we are his workmanship, created in Christ Jesus for good works, which God prepared beforehand, that we should walk in them.*

Ephesians 2:1-10

The Gospel According To Esther

....In the evening she would go in, and in the morning she would return to the second harem...

Esther 2:13

What are we to think about a book of the Bible with a heroine who compromised like Esther? Does my question offend you? I am not trying to be antagonistic. The problem is that many of us grew up cutting our teeth in Sunday school hearing about the morals of Esther. As a result, I am concerned that we don't really know the Esther story.

Let's review: Esther lived in Susa, hid her identity as a child of God, blended into Persia, submitted to its rules, and slept with the pagan king. At this point, we should not be reading Esther thinking, *let's follow her courageous example.* Rather, we should be alarmed by her actions.

Perhaps you don't like my take on Esther. I find many people want to press morals onto the pages of the Bible that aren't there. People like to make light of Joseph's brothers because, after all, it was God's plan and it worked out good for Joseph. Or we force a godliness onto Abraham by excusing his lies. After all, who could blame him?[51] Some like to point to David and his faith and courage in slaying Goliath while minimizing his adultery and murder. Have you noticed that the Bible seems more comfortable with the immorality of its so called heroes and heroines than we are? We look past their flaws in an effort to find fully sanctified role models. After all, we like our Bible heroes to be people who *deserve* to be found within the pages of God's Word. Instead, we find people like Peter, who denied Christ even when forewarned. What are we to think of a heroine who had unmarried sex with a pagan king? Tim Keller states in a sermon on Esther:

> *Esther gets to her pinnacle, her perch, through absolute compliance. Esther is completely compliant, she is the baby doll. She becomes the Barbie doll, she becomes the sex kitten. She does everything the men want her to do. Through completely selling out to the world's system, and making an idol out of feminine beauty and sexual prowess, and so on, she gets to her top perch.[52]*

I find Keller's words to be appropriately blunt and honest given what we read. The pagan king was not virtuous and it seems that Esther fully bought into the Empire's values. Some would say she was a victim and didn't have a choice. We can only speculate about her options. Additionally, I am not under the pretense that I could have handled things better than Esther or Mordecai! However, we know Daniel, under the threat of death, refused to submit to pagan Babylon. This posture landed him in the lion's den. Furthermore, Joseph rejected the advances of Pharaoh's wife which rewarded him with an Egyptian prison. The truth is that the Bible is not a book of

---

[51] On two occasions, Abraham said of his wife, Sarah, "she is my sister." This allowed Pharaoh and king Abimelech to send for her and take her. See Genesis 12 and 20.

[52] For further study I recommend these sermons by Tim Keller: http://www.gospelinlife.com/esther-and-the-hiddenness-of-god

morals; it is a book of mercy! That is the glory of God's Word! The Bible reveals people as they truly are. If we came to the Bible only to find perfectly moral followers of God, we would be utterly discouraged! Mercy isn't needed for heroes and heroines who are already sanctified. Mercy is for sinners. That is good news for people like us who peer into its pages! The glory of the book of Esther is that God was merciful to the imperfect people of God then and He is merciful to imperfect people today!

Yes, Mordecai and Esther should have left Susa. And yes, their decision to remain led to compromise. Nonetheless, God sovereignly used them to usher in His redemption plan. In the same fashion, our failures in following Christ has not written us out of the story of the mercy of God. He remains faithful! They should have run for their lives and they should not have denied their identity. But even still, the mercy of God rained down on them and showers of mercy rain on us as well! Christ is the hero in Esther and He, not us, is the hero in our lives! The apostle Paul helps us to see how God is the hero of our salvation story.

*"...even as **he chose** us in him before the foundation of the world, that we should be holy and blameless before him. **In love he** predestined us for adoption to himself as sons through Jesus Christ, **according to the purpose of his will, to the praise of his glorious grace...**"*

Ephesians 1:4-6

Here was the problem and the solution there in Susa: Esther was beautiful. However, the one thing more beautiful than Esther in all of Susa was the sovereign hand of God! Yes, God made her beautiful; but physical beauty was not God's ultimate goal. God was doing a work that was making her radiance to be more than skin deep!

We could say that, in one sense, Esther is not yet beautiful. She has a beautiful appearance but her actions are far from attractive. It is here that we might find ourselves under a mountain of discouragement if we think that the book is about Esther. Be encouraged, God is the King who does not banish his bride from His presence. Nor does He seek after her replacement.

Amazingly, when God seeks to describe the relationship He has with His people, He points to marriage. The bride of Christ, the church, doesn't go through endless beauty treatments prior to being brought before *the* King. No amount of beauty treatments would suffice for sin has left us hopelessly marred before a holy God. However, God our King does not reject his bride even in her remaining un-beautiful state. Christ's love was not based on Esther's created, outward, beauty; it was based on the beauty of the glory of Christ. This is the hope we find in Esther: We too are not yet beautiful but Christ is the faithful Groom who is committed to our growth in Him. For His glory, He is making us beautiful. He will never leave us or forsake us. He continues to love and refine the church, His bride.

.... as Christ loved the church and gave himself up for her, that he might sanctify her, having cleansed her by the washing of water with the word, so that he might present the church to himself in splendor, without spot or wrinkle or any such thing, that she might be holy and without blemish.

Ephesians 5:25-27

"For He who began a good work in you, will bring it to completion at the day of Jesus Christ."

Philippians 1:6

Ahasuerus displayed his wealth, power, and desired to display his wife, Vashti. Esther became a different kind of display for the King of kings. Both king Ahasuerus and King Jesus desire to display the beauty of their bride. One king demands beauty in his bride while the other King makes his bride beautiful. That is the glory we see unfolding in Esther. God was making Esther become the *showcase* of His providence, the glorious *display* of His mercy!

Aren't you glad that God's favorable providence is not determined by our wavering morality? Rather, it is firmly rooted in the unchanging character of God! We do not earn God's gracious providence. God wasn't waiting to work in Susa until Esther was sanctified. Furthermore, God didn't wait to move in us until we finally cleaned up our lives. We might call this *the gospel according to Esther.* The book of Esther points us to Jesus. He died because we cannot make ourselves beautiful!

> *For our sake he made him to be sin who knew no sin, so that in him we might become the righteousness of God.*
>
> *2 Corinthians 5:21*

Behold your God who has providentially saved you, in spite of you. The glory of salvation does not point to our moralism; the glory of salvation points to the perfect righteousness of Christ! Mordecai and Esther were unfaithful and yet, God chose to use them for the saving of lives. God is going to have a people. The redemptive storyline continued and it still continues through us today. This is the glory of the book of Esther: God sovereignly moved, in spite of them, to save them and eventually save us!

> *"...there are two great surprises in the world: that God has loved us so much, and that we in return continue to love him and trust him so little. May God increasingly press into our hearts the reality of the gospel, until our whole beings burn with passionate love for Him!"* [53]

Behold the hero of the book of Esther, our faithful, sovereign God!

Reflections:

- How were you taught the Esther story?

- When we press a morality onto the life of Esther, how does that belittle the glory of God's work in the Esther story?

- Consider your salvation story, how do you tell it? Do you make yourself or God the hero of the story?

---

[53] Iain M. Duguid. Esther & Ruth (Reformed Expository Commentary) (Kindle Locations 612-613). Kindle Edition.

Chapter 6: There was a king; There is a King

There was a king,
There is a King!
There was a kingdom,
There is a Kingdom.
The king had a glory that is no more,
Thee King is glorious forevermore!
He reigned then,
He reigns today.
Always was,
He always will be.
The Book of Esther is about THE KING whose reign never ends!

There Was A king

As Esther 2 comes to a close, we find Mordecai sitting at the king's gate where he eavesdropped on a private conversation. Some might call it coincidence but, rest assured, this happenstance was a glorious providence.

Presumably, Mordecai found himself at the king's gate because he had official duties of some sort or, perhaps, he was concerned for Esther's well being. Either way, while hanging around the king's gate, Mordecai heard a plot among the eunuchs to kill the king. Esther had been raised under Mordecai's protection but she was now under the rule of the pagan king. I wonder if Mordecai was tempted to lay low and let the plot to kill the king run its course. Instead, Mordecai revealed the plot and we might expect to read that he was greatly rewarded for doing so. However, no reward was offered, not even a pat on the back came as a result! The book marches on as the eunuchs were exposed and hung on the gallows and the whole episode was written in "the book of the chronicles" (2:23). That's right, stuffed away in a soon-to-be forgotten old and dusty history book.

70

There Is A King!

Oh, the glories of this little book called Esther! As God remains hidden on the surface, we have the opportunity to peer into the story and gain a wide angle view of how God faithfully works to redeem His people. Yes, there was a king in Susa. He was a lustful king who abducted young women out of their homes, making one his bride and the rest a part of his harem. There was another King in Susa. Though He was seemingly absent, He cannot be missed! Mordecai exposed the assassination plot and was overlooked by the king. Yet, he was never neglected by *the* King! Rest assured, if you are a child of the King, you too have never once been overlooked by *the* King!

We must realize that this seemingly accidental encounter at the king's gate was anything but accidental. It is none other than the providence of God. Webster's 1828 dictionary defines providence as it relates to theology as:

> *...the care and superintendence which God exercises over his creatures. He that acknowledges a creation and denies a providence involves himself in a palpable contradiction; for the same power which caused a thing to exist is necessary to continue its existence. Some persons admit a general providence but deny a particular providence not considering that a general providence consists of particulars. A belief in divine providence is a source of great consolation to good men.*[54]

Mordecai was in the right place at the right time to overhear the assassination plot because the sovereign God was actively being faithful to His covenants of promise.

An Unjust Promotion

Purim is the yearly commemoration of the defeat of Haman's plot to massacre the Jews. It was celebrated this year beginning on the evening of March 11th and ended the evening of March 12th. If

---

[54] http://webstersdictionary1828.com/Dictionary/Providence

you are not a Jew, you may have heard of Purim but you might not know its significance.[55] The word Purim comes from the Hebrew word for "lots." In Esther 9, we see Haman casting lots to determine the day to execute the Jews. Let's peer into Haman's rise and fall that is celebrated every year during Purim.

After these things, King Ahasuerus promoted Haman the Agagite, the son of Hammedatha, and advanced him and set his throne above all the officials who were with him. And all the king's servants who were at the king's gate bowed down and paid homage to Haman...

Esther 3:1-2

Can you hear Mordecai shout from the pages of Esther, *"No, not Haman the Agagite! Anyone but him! My arch enemy, the one who is the biggest thorn in my side, just received the promotion I deserved for unveiling the plot I unearthed!*

What was it like for Mordecai to see homage being given to his enemy? Even worse, what was it like to watch his Jewish brothers and sisters bowing to Haman *the Agagite*? Perhaps this idolatrous worship was the catalyst that snapped Mordecai out of the trance Susa held on him.

Chapter breaks often get in the way of a correct reading of God's Word. These divisions are not a part of the inspired Word. They tend to break our flow of thought, creating an unhelpful divide. As one chapter ends, our minds tend to shut down as a new chapter begins. However, if we re-read the end of chapter two and the beginning of chapter three without the chapter break, I think we will feel the sting of this moment as it was originally intended.

*And this came to the knowledge of Mordecai, and he told it to Queen Esther, and Esther told the king in the name of Mordecai. When the affair was investigated and found to be so, the men were both hanged on the gallows. And it was recorded in the book of the chronicles in the presence of the king. **After these things King Ahasuerus***

---

[55] Purim is the Jewish festival held in spring (on the 14th or 15th day of Adar).

promoted Haman the Agagite, the son of Hammedatha, and advanced him and set his throne above all the officials who were with him.

Esther 2:22-3:1

Did you hear it? Can you feel Mordecai's angst? Perhaps, in the sovereign mercy of God, God brought about the promotion of Haman to wake up comfortable Mordecai. It wouldn't be the first or last time God would do such a thing. Are we to think the fate of Mordecai and the promotion of Haman was an oversight a mere cosmic accident? Do we think that God was wringing His hands, frantically trying to devise a new plan to redeem His people? On the contrary, God had His eyes on something bigger than Mordecai's promotion. In the economy of God, He views our redemption to be valued more highly than our promotion.

Have you known the sting of Mordecai's non-promotion? You played along with the king's games and followed the rules of the empire as you worked hard to advance yourself, giving so much to the job, arriving early and staying late. As you strived harder than everyone around you, you were certain the promotion belonged to you. But the position along with the raise went to the other person, the one who backstabbed and manipulated to land the breakthrough you felt you had earned. The elevated role went to the person who made it known that your God-talk was repulsive. Now, your newly promoted boss regularly mocks the God you love. Unbelievably, a type of homage is now owed him. Imagine you're Mordecai. You gave up your cousin to be the queen of a selfish and angry king. You then unveiled the plot to assassinate the king and what did you get in response? Your enemy, Haman, was promoted to rule over you! What a nightmare!

Are you able to see the hand of God in the injustice? Is it conceivable that God might be at work in the unfair promotion? Maybe the values of the King are vastly different than ours. Is it possible the King has positioned you for something more valuable than a pay raise or a better lifestyle? Look around your workplace. God may not be on the lips of the people at your place of employment. Yet, Esther teaches us to trust that God is at work. Have you noticed it is far easier to memorize and quote Romans 8:28 than it is to trust Romans 8:28?

And we know that for those who love God all things work together for good, for those who are called according to his purpose.

Romans 8:28

Do you have a category for not receiving the promotion you deserve? Do you find yourself praising God or accusing Him, trusting or fearing? Perhaps God has fallen asleep at the wheel, isn't sovereign, is uncaring, or is unfaithful. Doesn't God know how much you needed that raise for vacationing? Or perhaps the lack of promotion is for the saving of lives. We don't typically think like that. Our immediate response struggles to consider the possible opportunities God has for us. We think too highly of the raise and not highly enough of the mission. As a result, we make our angry demands upon God and call it "prayer." God clearly doesn't get it. Why has God not rewarded my honesty and hard work? He has obviously missed how hard we worked for the promotion.

For my thoughts are not your thoughts, neither are your ways my ways, declares the LORD. For as the heavens are higher than the earth, so are my ways higher than your ways and my thoughts than your thoughts.

Isaiah 55:8-9

We nod our head in agreement and proclaim an "amen" to the preacher as he unpacks Paul's thorn, Joseph's prison, or Mordecai's lack of promotion while we bristle with God's so called "higher ways" in our lives. Esther shows us that even when God is not named in the secular empire of Susa, He is orchestrating events to bring about the salvation of His people! Maybe our country's failing government, crumbling economy, diving morality, or our personal sufferings exist for the saving of lives. Is it possible you work where you work for more than a paycheck? Is it possible that work is for something more than what we have been told: "be fulfilled and do

74

something you love?" Might it be that you suffer, the way you suffer, for redemptive reasons? While we may not know all that God is up to in our lives; Esther shows us that we can trust Him! C.S. Lewis states it like this: *"Every disability conceals a vocation, if only we can find it, which will turn the necessity to glorious gain."*

God is a God on a mission. We need not look any further than the cross to see the mission of God. Christ did not deserve to be crucified but God the Father was not seeking what the Son deserved; He was seeking our redemption. The cross tells us that we can trust Him. He is faithful!

A Turn For The Worse!

And when Haman saw that Mordecai did not bow down or pay homage to him, Haman was filled with fury. But he disdained to lay hands on Mordecai alone. So, as they had made known to him the people of Mordecai, **Haman sought to destroy all the Jews, the people of Mordecai, throughout the whole kingdom of Ahasuerus.**

Esther 3:5-6

"All the king's servants" were bowing down and paying homage to Haman. But our friend Mordecai refused to submit. Now Haman sought to not only destroy his enemy Mordecai but also all the Jews living in Persia! I have been painting Mordecai as a guy who should have known better than to remain in Susa and conceal his identity. While Mordecai had been weak and cowardly, God had been merciful, faithful, redeeming, and sovereign. In Esther 3 Mordecai shifted and made a bold move in the right direction. *"Hey, guys I have been a passive follower of God. I have been living in and of the world of Susa, but I won't bow and pay homage to Haman, and by the way, I also will not continue to suppress who I am - I am a Jew!"*

And when they spoke to him day after day and he would not listen to them, they told Haman, in order to see whether Mordecai's words would stand, **for he had told them that he was a Jew.**

Esther 3:4

75

Mordecai threw down the gauntlet! That is what God's mercy provokes in our lives. We can all recall times of passivity, moving in and settling into our Susa, comfortably living in this world when God, in His mercy, awoke us from our slumber. His grace moves us to devotion, calling us to pray and leading us to live visibly for *the* King.

Are you falling in love with this little book called Esther? Are you seeing that the faithfulness and mercy of God in your life today is not all that different than God's faithfulness and mercy in the lives of His people so many years ago? Flowing from that fountain of mercy, I pray that God might root us in our convictions. Don't bow to the pressures and the gods of this age!

For many years abortion bothered me but it didn't provoke me. I voted for policies that agreed with my conviction but, at the same time, I was living in the comfortable land of Susa. *Suppress who you are Tim, cave to the pressure of Susa.* I was obscuring who I was and bowing to the pressures of the kingdom. Fortunately, quite a few years ago God revealed to me my passive posture. Since then I have sought to "not bow." God in His mercy convicted me while reading sermons by John Piper and others.[56] Today I desire to be a caring voice, a voice that speaks both truth and grace. I have sought to be a supporter of those who are on the front-lines of caring for people who may be considering abortion or have already gone through the emotional pains of an abortion.[57]

How about you? In what ways might you be caving to the pressures of this world? Perhaps God is using the book of Esther to wake you up from your slumber. If so, be encouraged! This is the faithful mercy of God!

---

[56] http://desiringgod.org

[57] If you are considering an abortion or if you are experiencing the hurt of a past abortion, please feel free to contact me. I would love to have the opportunity to point you to friends who truly care and desire to help you. http://melbournepri.com

Consider the landscape as Mordecai turned and took his stand. Mordecai was one man, the one man that refused to bow. In retribution for injured pride, Haman began to plan the annihilation of *all* the Jews across the entire empire. We might think that Mordecai's good actions would bring about a favorable set of circumstances. Have you experienced this? Having turned from sin, one might assume that things will get better but often they get worse. After all, now we think we *deserve* better. We always seem to try to bring our good works into the equation. Sinclair Ferguson writes;

"The glory of the gospel is that God has declared Christians to be rightly related to him in spite of their sin. But our greatest temptation and mistake is to try to smuggle character into his work of grace. How easily we fall into the trap of assuming that we remain justified only so long as there are grounds in our character for our justification."[58]

Whenever we begin to think we *deserve* something, we have begun that "smuggling of character into his work of grace," that Ferguson describes. God is the faithful, merciful, redeeming, sovereign King. He is not the, "make everything easy" King. God is up to something eternally bigger than simply making our lives comfortable and prosperous. There is a bigger agenda: God is saving lives through Mordecai and through us! This higher agenda reminds us of Paul to the Philippians as he seeks to encourage the saints in Philippi.

I want you to know, brothers, that what has happened to me has really served to advance the gospel, so that it has become known throughout the whole imperial guard and to all the rest that my imprisonment is for Christ. And most of the brothers, having become confident in the Lord by my imprisonment, are much more bold to speak the word without fear.

Philippians 1:12-14

---

[58] Sinclair B. Ferguson, Banner of Truth, 2013,The Christian Life: A Doctrinal Introduction, pages 82-83

Paul views his arrest as a good thing when it means the Gospel is advancing! Who is your God? Do you have a category for a Sovereign God who allows things to grow worse when you are finally getting things right? Life became increasingly difficult for Mordecai and sometimes life becomes increasingly difficult for us too. When it does, we can trust God with the details of our lives. God is at work using our suffering to grow us and redeem others!

The king's Decree

*Then Haman said to King Ahasuerus, "There is a certain people scattered abroad and dispersed among the peoples in all the provinces of your kingdom. Their laws are different from those of every other people, and they do not keep the king's laws, so that it is not to the king's profit to tolerate them. If it please the king, **let it be decreed that they be destroyed.***

Esther 3:8-9

The king handed Haman his ring and told him to do with the Jews whatever he thought best. Thus, the decree was issued that sealed the fate of the Jews. Imagine the horror as the people read the edict: *"Annihilate all Jews, young and old, women and children..."* Did Mordecai wonder if he should have allowed the plot to the kill the king to go unhindered? The people of God were now under an edict of death. As the decree reached the ears of the Jews, they responded in fasting, weeping, and lamenting. Many of them could be found lying in sackcloth and ashes, which was an appropriate response to grief. According to Persian law, the king's decree could not be changed. The most powerful man on the face of the earth had sealed their fate. These were dark days, as there was no hope for the Jews living in this kingdom.

The King's Decree

There is another King living in Susa and He has made a few decrees of His own!

Now the LORD said to Abram, "Go from your country and your
kindred and your father's house to the land that I will show you. And I
will make of you a great nation, and I will bless you and make your
name great, so that you will be a blessing. I will bless those who bless
you, and him who dishonors you I will curse, and in you all the
families of the earth shall be blessed. "

Genesis 12:1-3

It is important for us to note that the decree of king Ahasuerus
was in direct opposition to the decree of *the* King. Whose decree will
stand? They can't both be adhered to. I am amazed as I consider that
the king of this world, Satan, has decreed our certain death. But that
decree was no match for the Savior's sacrifice! Whose decree will
win out? Thanks be to God, His decrees are everlasting!

For the wages of sin is death...(this is the decree that hangs over
sinners. And yet, there is more to the decree of our King)
but the free gift of God is eternal life in Christ Jesus our Lord.
Romans 6:23

Praise be to *the* King! He has decreed a gift of eternal life
through His Son. This edict of *the* King is unchangeable. Behold the
god in the book of Esther, king Ahasuerus, who ruled the mighty
Persian empire. And behold our God, The King of kings, who
continues to rule over all of creation! Unlike king Ahasuerus, the
Lord is infinitely wise, just, faithful and good. Because He is holy
and just, He must uphold His righteous decrees! But, unlike king
Ahasuerus, His decree was not made out of ignorance and haste; it
was made before the foundation of the world!

Blessed be the God and Father of our Lord Jesus Christ, who has
blessed us in Christ with every spiritual blessing in the heavenly
places, even as he chose us in him before the foundation of the world,
that we should be holy and blameless before him. In love he
predestined us for adoption as sons through Jesus Christ, according
to the purpose of his will, to the praise of his glorious grace, with
which he has blessed us in the Beloved. In him we have redemption
through his blood, the forgiveness of our trespasses, according to the

79

riches of his grace, which he lavished upon us, in all wisdom and insight making known to us the mystery of his will, according to his purpose, which he set forth in Christ as a plan for the fullness of time, to unite all things in him, things in heaven and things on earth. In him we have obtained an inheritance, having been predestined according to the purpose of him who works all things according to the counsel of his will, so that we who were the first to hope in Christ might be to the praise of his glory. In him you also, when you heard the word of truth, the gospel of your salvation, and believed in him, were sealed with the promised Holy Spirit, who is the guarantee of our inheritance until we acquire possession of it, to the praise of his glory.

Ephesians 1:3-14

Haman was not given the honor he thought was due him. And when Haman was not honored, the king was not honored. This lack of honor is what brought Ahasuerus to this decree of death. The irony we are to see is that *the* King was not honored in Esther. Esther and the Jews in Susa bowed their knees to another king. They signed up for Susa and all that went with it. What was the response of *the* King of kings? Did he annihilate His people in Susa by allowing the king's decree to stand? The response of *the* King of kings then and now is faithfulness and mercy!

Mercy Between Brothers

Two brothers could be heard in the back yard as they playfully fought with each other. The older brother finally had the upper hand as he landed with all his weight on his little brother's belly. Pinning down his arms he shouted, "Say mercy!" The smaller and younger brother yelled in reply "Nooooooo!" "Okay then," came the older brother's response, "the punishments will continue!" At that point, the older brother began to *mercilessly* inflict the ultimate weapon: tickling. Across the neighborhood, cries were heard from the younger boy as he shouted, "mercy, mercy, M E R C Y!!" The older brother relented. They helped each other up cleaning the dirt off their backs when, suddenly, the little brother initiated "The Rematch." That event played out countless times for me and my older brother, Jeff.

While it's a fun game for kids, it is serious business for sinners. Mercy is compassion. It is forgiveness offered when the power to inflict punishment is available. Our God is a merciful God! We have greatly wronged Him who has the power to inflict punishment upon us. And yet, for those who repent of their sins and trust in Him for the forgiveness of sins, he offers us His mercy!

Both decrees of the kings were to be heralded. King Ahasuerus' decree was to be proclaimed and the news was to be spread across the empire. The announcement went out: *death to the people of God, the Jews.*

It is marvelous to consider that we too have been commissioned to spread the news across the world. This proclamation of death includes the offer of a new life. The Lord's decree has gone out, the death sentence has been declared; sinners are in need of a Savior! In God's mercy and faithfulness, He raised up Esther as a savior to His people in Susa. What's more, He sent His Son to be our Savior, redeeming His people today! Another decree is to be shouted from the mountain top. It is not the proclamation of the death of a people; we are to proclaim the death of *the* King! We proclaim Christ crucified to a world that stands under the decree of sin and death. It is a decree of life-giving hope in the face of certain death. Let the world know: we were to die but *the* King died for us. Praise to *the* King!

Reflections:

- In what ways has this chapter adjusted your perspective of being passed over for a promotion you thought you deserved?

- How is God calling you to trust in His providence, even when you might not be seeing Him actively moving in the circumstances of your life?

Chapter 7: **Gospel Shadows**

"The kingdom of God is not of the people, by the people, or for the people. It is a kingdom ruled by a King, and God does not rule by the consent of His subjects but by His sovereign authority. His reign extends over me whether I vote for Him or not."

R.C. Sproul

Alfred Hitchcock had a gift for unpacking a story like none other. Known for his twisted endings, he earned the title: "The Master Of Suspense." I always enjoyed seeing his plump face and balding head as he made a brief cameo in each of his movies. He might be found at the back of a bus, a random face in a crowd, or pictured on a newspaper advertisement promoting a new weight loss medicine. It was his trademark, a way for him to put his signature on his movies. It's a moment of humor and a brief *shadow* of the man, that masterful creator of suspense.

Esther Is Not The Savior

As mentioned earlier, all of the Bible is about Jesus. You could say that the Old Testament is a shadow of the One who is yet to come. Therefore, Esther is a type of savior, standing in a long line of previous deliverers. People like Joseph, Moses, Gideon, Samson, Ruth, and others were used by God to accomplish the salvation of His people. However, Esther is not *the* Savior; she is a shadow, a foreshadowing of the ultimate Redeemer. Consider a few similarities between the Esther story and Jesus:

Both Esther and Jesus were raised far from home: Esther in Susa, having forsaken community in Jerusalem and Jesus on fallen earth, declined the comforts of Heaven.

...though he was in the form of God, did not count equality with God a thing to be grasped, but emptied himself, by taking the form of a servant, being born in the likeness of men.

Philippians 2:6-7

Both Esther and Jesus were adopted and raised by a father who was not their biological relative. They both grew up in humble circumstances and relative insignificance. Humanly speaking, they were both implausible choices for ushering in God's salvation plan. Women were not valued in the ancient culture, making Esther a very unlikely savior. And clearly, Jesus was not what this world was looking for in a savior. Consider how the prophet Isaiah spoke of Jesus with such unflattering descriptions.

...had no form or majesty that we should look at him, and no beauty that we should desire him. He was despised and rejected by men, a man of sorrows and acquainted with grief; and as one from whom men hide their faces he was despised, and we esteemed him not.

Isaiah 53:2-3

Religious leaders who were well versed in Scripture entirely discarded Jesus. An unlikely Savior indeed! Both Jesus and Esther went before the world's most powerful leaders to usher in the salvation of God's people from certain death. Esther's performance before the king won the favor of the king, freeing God's people from undoubtable death. Similarly, Christ's performance won the favor of *the* King of all kings, also saving us from certain death!

Sovereignty And Responsibility

When Mordecai learned all that had been done, Mordecai tore his clothes and put on sackcloth and ashes, and went out into the midst of the city, and he cried out with a loud and bitter cry. He went up to the entrance of the king's gate, for no one was allowed to enter the king's gate clothed in sackcloth. And in every province, wherever the king's command and his decree reached, **there was great mourning among** **the Jews, with fasting and weeping and lamenting, and many of** **them lay in sackcloth and ashes.** *When Esther's young women and her eunuchs came and told her, the queen was deeply distressed. She sent garments to clothe Mordecai, so that he might take off his sackcloth, but he would not accept them.*

Esther 4:1-4

While Esther is not the Savior, she does carry a responsibility. Throughout the book of Esther God is revealed to be sovereignly working behind the scenes to bring about his good purposes, He is pleased to do so through the activity of His everyday people. There is much to benefit when we wrestle with God's sovereignty and our responsibility. This wrestling helps us to grow in our faith in the Lord as we seek to live for Him. That said, while we wrestle with God's sovereignty and our responsibility, it is important to note that the Bible doesn't. God's Word is content to simply state it as is and without conflict. We would prefer to know where God's sovereignty and our responsibilities begin and end. The Word, however, writes God's sovereignty and man's responsibility into the same story, indeed, often in the same verse.[59] That is what we find in Esther 4.

The first thing we are to note is that the believer who firmly accepts the sovereign hand of God is not passive. Passive Christianity is an oxymoron, plain and simple. As the redeemed people of God, we are called to do the Lord's work the Lord's way as we seek to obey God's will for our lives. Motivated by the mercy of the Gospel, we are spurred into joyful action that is empowered and guided by the Holy Spirit. All this activity is under the sovereign hand of God. The Gospel must be more to us than an intellectual assent; it is power for transformation. The Gospel calls us to live in the good of all that it provides. To live in the good of the Gospel is to be propelled forward into active involvement in His plan of redemption![60]

---

[59] A few quick examples of man's responsibility and God's sovereignty: Philippians 3:12-13, Acts 4:27-28, 1 Corinthians 12.

[60] For further study on this topic I recommend: https://www.9marks.org/article/gospel-implications/ or download Mike Bullmore's sermon The Functional Centrality Of The Gospel

Accordingly, we have seen a shift in Mordecai as he let it be known that he was a Jew. Furthermore, in Esther 4 Mordecai was found in sackcloth and ashes, weeping loudly at the king's gate. Typically, one would grieve in this manner after a death had occurred. But in this case, we see Mordecai grieving preemptively. This early grief displayed the impending doom and absolute hopelessness of the moment.

It was wholly inappropriate to clothe oneself in this grief at the king's gate. If Mordecai was seeking Esther's attention, it worked. Given his actions, it is likely that Esther feared for Mordecai's safety. Remember, appearances play a major role in Esther so she sends the appropriate clothing to Mordecai, which he promptly refused. Prior to this point we have seen opulent displays of wealth, been told of Vashti's and Esther's beauty, and have been given details about the year long beauty treatments. With those images as our backdrop, we now see the contrasting appearance of a pitiful weeping man, dressed in sackcloth at the king's gate.

These were important actions taken by Mordecai that drew Esther out of her passivity. While their activity was important, they were not needed. How can I say they were important *and* not needed? Identically, we might ask: is it man's responsibility or God's sovereignty? It is both. However, let's not hold to the false notion that God *needs* us.

"Do not think to yourself that in the king's palace you will escape any more than all the other Jews. For if you keep silent at this time, relief and deliverance will rise for the Jews from another place...And who knows whether you have not come to the kingdom for such a time as this?"

Esther 4:13-14

Mordecai was right, if Esther did not act, relief and deliverance would come from somewhere else. While man's actions could be taken out of the equation, God's actions cannot be removed. If Mordecai and/or Esther were not in Susa, God could have sovereignly raised up another deliverer. However, if God was not in

Susa, neither the actions by Mordecai nor the position of Esther would have made the slightest difference. Let us not go on inflating ourselves by thinking that God is in need of us. Indeed, we are the needy ones. Imagine for a moment our fate if it were not for the constant, steady and sovereign hand of our King!

Behold Your Mediator

Webster's 1828 Dictionary defines Mediator as such,

> **MEDIATOR**, Noun
>
> One that interposes between parties at variance for the purpose of reconciling them.
>
> By way of eminence, Christ is the mediator the divine intercessor through whom sinners may be reconciled to an offended God. I Tim. 2:5.
>
> Christ is a mediator by nature, as partaking of both natures divine and human; and mediator by office, as transacting matters between God and man.[61]

Esther, the mediator, went before the king to make her appeal on behalf of the doomed Jews. Amazingly, God used a compromising, pretty Jewish girl to accomplish His purposes. God's sovereign grace was greater than all of her failures. Likewise, His faithfulness overrides our half-hearted desires to serve Him. This is a glorious assurance to the Christian who lives aware of his or her failures. Behold the glory of Esther and the glorious story of every believer in Jesus Christ! Sinful man is in desperate need of a divine mediator to save him/her from utter destruction. Christ came to be the perfect Mediator, saving us from the death our sins deserved!

Mordecai understood that the Jews needed the queen to risk her life and represent them before the king. The Jews were unaware that before they were under the decree of death, and before they

---

[61] http://webstersdictionary1828.com/Dictionary/mediator

began to fast, God had already positioned Esther to go before the king. Unbeknownst to them, their answer was already in place!

Was not this helplessness our state prior to coming to Christ? We might have been remotely aware of our unrighteousness before God. We might have even known that something needed to be done. Like the Jews in Susa, we were unaware that God had already answered our dilemma. Before you and I ever were, God the Father sent a Mediator, and positioned Him to bring about our salvation! What a glorious day when God opened our eyes to see the Mediator and realized all that He had done to accomplish our redemption! While Esther, the mediator, was reluctant to approach the king, there was no reluctance in our Mediator. Jesus Christ joyfully went to the cross!

Therefore, since we are surrounded by so great a cloud of witnesses, let us also lay aside every weight, and sin which clings so closely, and let us run with endurance the race that is set before us, looking to Jesus, the founder and perfecter of our faith, who for the joy that was set before him endured the cross, despising the shame, and is seated at the right hand of the throne of God.

Hebrews 12:1-2

For there is one God, and there is one mediator between God and men, the man Christ Jesus, who gave himself as a ransom for all, which is the testimony given at the proper time.

I Timothy 2:5-6

Mordecai understood Esther's dilemma and yet he remained unmoved by her prospect of death. Esther 4:13-14 is as close as the book of Esther will get to referencing the hand of God. Unsurprisingly, the author remained one step short of mentioning divine activity.

"...relief and deliverance will come... And who knows whether you have not come to the kingdom for such a time as this?"

Esther 4:14

"Who knows....?" That is the extent of Mordecai's faith. Without mentioning God, Mordecai was theologically correct. Relief would come because God is God in Susa. RC Sproul states, *"If there is one single molecule in this universe running around loose, totally free of God's sovereignty, then we have no guarantee that a single promise of God will ever be fulfilled."* If God is not sovereign, then God is not God. Sweet Providence, our King was directing every minuscule detail for His glory and His people's salvation. Likewise, "For such a time as this...." Christ our Mediator came at the God-ordained time to rescue us!

But when the fullness of time had come, God sent forth his Son, born of woman, born under the law, to redeem those who were under the law, so that we might receive adoption as sons.

Galatians 4:4-5

Christ restored life and peace between a holy God and a sinful race. Mordecai persuaded Esther to go before the king under the threat of death. Our Savior needed no such persuasion! Christ, our Mediator, willingly and knowingly went before the Father to atone for our sins. Esther's death was a possibility, Christ's death was a certainty.

*"Then Esther told them to reply to Mordecai, "Go, gather all the Jews to be found in Susa, and hold a fast on my behalf, and do not eat or drink for three days, night or day. I and my young women will also fast as you do. **Then I will go to the king, though it is against the law, and if I perish, I perish."***

Esther 4:14-15

From that time Jesus began to show his disciples that he must go to Jerusalem and suffer many things from the elders and chief priests and scribes, and be killed, and on the third day be raised.

Matthew 16:21

Not only did the appearances shift in Susa but the feasting did as well. Feasting held a place of priority in Susa. The book began with the king's feast. Vashti even held an exclusive feast for the women. Esther will be inviting the king to a feast and the book will end in a feast. But nestled between these feasts is a fast. The story carries us along feasting, then fasting, and then it concludes in feasting. This cycle too is reflective of the Christian life. Let there be feasting and fasting that will one day culminate at the feast of the marriage supper of the Lamb!

*Then I heard what seemed to be the voice of a great multitude, like the roar of many waters and like the sound of mighty peals of thunder, crying out, "Hallelujah! For the Lord our God the Almighty reigns. Let us rejoice and exult and give him the glory, For the marriage of the Lamb has come, And his Bride has made herself ready; it was granted her to clothe herself with fine linen, bright and pure"—for the fine linen is the righteous deeds of the saints. And the angel said to me, "Write this: **Blessed are those who are invited to the marriage supper of the Lamb.**"*

Revelation 19:6-9

Prayer And Fasting

Interestingly, a fast was called in Susa while prayer went unmentioned. Once again, the author (or Author, if you prefer) leaves us one step short by not mentioning prayer. We might assume prayer was a part of the fast. Nonetheless, the text is saying something by not saying *"prayer and fasting."* Certainly, this omission was not an oversight. The author intentionally continues to lead us along, even as the fasting and their actions lacked any recognition of God!

We would all do well to not leave prayer off the pages of our lives. Have you found that you think about prayer more than you pray? Or that you think you pray more than you actually pray? Let's try to insert ourselves into Susa and fast and pray. Pushing aside our failures, shortcomings, and discouragements, let us pray!

This is Mordecai's moment. *"And who knows whether you have not come to the kingdom for such a time as this?"* Additionally, perhaps God has placed you exactly where He has you. Is it possible that your move across the country was for something more than a career change? Perhaps the move has left you considering your responsibilities more than God's sovereignty. Is it possible that God has not answered your prayers like you desire because He has other plans for you? We are to read Esther and realize that none of us are where we are merely by *our actions*. God is at work! He is *the* King in Susa and He is *the* King wherever you call home. Once again, RC Sproul is helpful when he states, "Most Christian's salute the sovereignty of God but believe in the sovereignty of man." Be convinced, God has placed you and positioned you for His purpose. This life is much bigger than our petty goals. We have been saved to then be sent as ambassadors of Christ![62]

Consider the contrasts between Esther and Mordecai. God gave an elevated position to Esther while He kept the deserving Mordecai from a promotion. Esther's promotion was due to her physical beauty and Mordecai's lack of promotion was an oversight of his character. It was God who made one to be queen and the other to be lower than his worst enemy. Both the elevation and the lack of promotion was from the sovereign hand of God! Our responsibility isn't to figure out or question these mysteries in our lives. Rather, our responsibility is to accept the promotion or the lack thereof as a gift from our Sovereign God, for the saving of lives. Friends, our lives are bigger than a paycheck. God is at work, redeeming His people in our Susa! You live, work, go to school, and attend a night class where you do because God placed you there for His sovereign purpose. Furthermore, Christ our mediator embraced His demotion of human flesh and the lowly cross to then be exalted by the Father. Behold your Mediator!

Royal Robes

At this point, Esther's beauty seems to have been set aside to show us the beauty of her actions and help us consider our own

---

[62] 2 Corinthians 5:20

responsibilities as we serve the Sovereign King. Esther had counted the cost, something Christ called all of His disciples to do. She had determined that the safety of her people was more important than her own comforts. Esther then prepared herself by gathering support from the community of her fellow Jews, calling on them to fast.

You and I will probably not be called upon to risk our very lives to save others. And yet, God has issued a radical call to each of us. We too are called to die to ourselves as we "go into all the world..."[63] This daily dying to self takes place in the coffee shop, grocery store, office, and school during seemingly mundane moments of life. Not unlike Esther, it is a death to our priorities and comforts for the sake of those who are under the decree of death. Though our circumstances are vastly different, we are inclined toward our own self-preservation in a similar manner as Esther.

On the third day Esther put on her royal robes....

Esther 5:1

When I am reading God's Word and I stumble upon "royal robes," it is a moment for me to slow down the reading. For instance, consider the prodigal son in Luke 15. The younger son had disrespected his father by asking for his inheritance while his father was living. This disrespect would not have gone unnoticed to Luke's original audience. In essence, the son was saying: *Father, I don't want you; I don't want a relationship with you; I only want what you can give me.* He opted to end the relationship with his father and instead asked for the things his father could offer him. The son then ran off and squandered the inheritance his father graciously gave him. We then find the young man eating among the pigs. While coming to his senses, he realized that his father's hired servants were better off than he was. He wised up and returned home to ask his father to allow him to become a hired hand. The father, however, had nothing to do with this "hired servant" nonsense. The father said to his servants:

---

[63] Matthew 28:19

Bring quickly the best robe, and put it on him, and put a ring on his hand, and shoes on his feet.

Luke 15:22

The "best robe" in the house would have been the father's robe. The father, in the face of the son's disrespect, is saying: *Clothe him not in the rags he was wearing, clothe him in the best robe, MY robe. Why? Because you are MY son, and all I have belongs to you. As my son, you will not be clothed in the filth you are wearing!"*

Unsurprisingly, we find Esther putting on her best robe. Why? Because she was going before the king and one would never go before the king dressed in everyday clothes. There is a beautiful shadow of the Gospel in these robes. We too have shrugged off a relationship with the Father, and instead, pursued Him for the things that He could offer us. The prodigal has come home and the Father has clothed us in the robes of Christ's righteousness. One day, all will stand before *the* King of kings. When we do, we will not be clothing ourselves in the robes of our good works! We would not dare go before *the* King wearing the "filthy rags" (Isaiah 64:6) of our efforts. Praise be to God! As we go before *the* King, we will be clothed in Christ's robes of perfect righteousness! The Father offers His prodigal sons and daughters His best robes. These robes are not earned. They are graciously given to prodigals through Christ's life and death on the cross![64]

The king's Inner Court

*Esther put on her royal robes **and stood in the inner court of the king's palace, in front of the king's quarters, while the king was sitting on his royal throne** inside the throne room opposite the entrance to the palace.*

Esther 5:1

---

[64] For a fuller treatment of the prodigal son check out Tim Keller's fantastic book titled The Prodigal God. To help your children understand this concept I recommend R.C. Sprouls excellent children's book: The Priest With Dirty Clothes.

Everything about the palace pointed to the glory of the king. Esther stood in the "inner court of the *king's* palace, in front of the *king's* quarters, while the *king* sat...."

Do you get the feel of this place? It was all about the king! It is said that wherever you found yourself in this inner court, you were viewing the king. The king was the center. Individuals were to behold his glory, power, and majesty. Consider the Old Testament tabernacle. Within the tabernacle was the Holy of Holies. One did not approach that holiest of places flippantly. The priest did not march into the presence of the Almighty God and the people knew they were to keep their distance. There was a curtain that separated that which was holy from that which was unclean. This separation was a reminder of the garden of Eden, as sin had separated us from God. To barge into the inner court meant death to unclean, sinful man. Likewise, Esther, aware of the king's majesty, did not boldly march into the presence of the king. Knees knocking and heart pounding, Esther approached the throne of the mighty king Ahasuerus. Fearing for her life, I would imagine that her request had been often rehearsed in privacy. Everything had to be just right, polished and perfect.

*And when the king saw Queen Esther standing in the court, **she won favor in his sight, and he held out to Esther the golden scepter that was in his hand. Then Esther approached...***

Esther 5:2

Rather than ending her life, he acted favorably towards her!

Approaching *the* King

Since then we have a great high priest who has passed through the heavens, Jesus, the Son of God, let us hold fast our confession. For we do not have a high priest who is unable to sympathize with our weaknesses, but one who in every respect has been tempted as we are, yet without sin. Let us then with confidence draw near to the throne of grace, that we may receive mercy and find grace to help in time of need.

Hebrews 4:14-16

Be freshly amazed at the glories Hebrews 4 is proclaiming. Those glories were certainly not missed by Hebrews' original audience. They knew their Scriptures, what we call the Old Testament. They knew one did not go boldly into the presence of God. What's changed? Because of the perfect life and death of Jesus on the cross, we may now approach God's throne! We do not come before the King today all polished and perfect; we do not confidently approach His throne impressed with our good deeds and dressed in our robes of morality. We come before the throne humbled. As wretched sinners, we come with no confidence in our good efforts. Rather, we are invited to come with confidence in the works of Jesus. As the great hymn, Rock of Ages, states it; "we come with His righteousness on." The invitation is to come in the confidence of what Christ has done on our behalf! We approach His throne, placing our faith in the perfect righteousness of Jesus.

You and I may approach the King today! It will cost us nothing but it was not free; the King paid the price through His death on the cross! Consider that day when we will stand before the very throne of the living God, *the* King of all kings. Because Christ purchased your salvation, you will not be condemned to an eternity apart from Him. You will receive "favor in his sight!" This wonderful glory brings us to worship the King!

Reflections:

- In what way is God moving you from a posture of passivity?

- Looking back on your salvation story, how was God at work bringing you to a place of repentance and faith?

Chapter 8: **Extraordinarily.... Ordinary**

"Facing another day, with ordinary callings to ordinary people all around us is much more difficult than chasing my own dreams that I have envisioned for the grand story of my life."

Michael S. Horton, Ordinary: Sustainable Faith in a Radical, Restless World

"Preach the gospel, die and be forgotten."

Nicholaus von Zinzendorf

At this point, a quick summary of Esther is needed to help us separate the trees from the forest. The king had banished Vashti and replaced her with a new queen, Esther, who happened to be a part of God's covenant people. Mordecai was at the right place at the right time when he overheard the plot to kill the king. Rather than receiving a promotion, Mordecai's arch enemy, Haman, received the reward Mordecai deserved. Haman lusted for the respect of Mordecai, demanding his submission and reverence but Mordecai refused. Haman overreacted by deceptively influencing the king to decree the death of all the Jews. Mordecai then told Esther of their impending death, at which time Esther explained to him that for her to go before the king might mean the death of her. Esther called for a fast and took an "if I die, I die" approach. Lastly, she invited the king and Haman to a private feast.

Here is what I love about the book of Esther: It is incredibly simple! The storyline flows in an extraordinarily-ordinary fashion.

The Red Sea will not split in two. There will be no manna from heaven, no flood, no shutting of the mouths of lions or the seemingly impossible slaying of a giant with a sling shot. As you read Esther, there aren't any miracles to report. Don't get me wrong. What we read is miraculous. But, in Esther, we see God doing the miraculous through the natural, everyday rhythms of life. A queen who was beautiful, a Jew, a feast, a plot overheard, a king who couldn't sleep, another feast, and so on.

Everyday, Ordinary, Woman

Do you see it? Can you spot how God was at work through natural means and yet He was at work in such a profound way? Esther was a normal young lady. Yes, she was beautiful but she was everyday beautiful. She was not angelic; there wasn't a halo or heavenly radiance that surrounded her. Nonetheless, we see the supernatural hand of God that was working through her. Do you question "if" God was at work in Esther? Am I stretching the meaning of Esther by placing God in the thick of the plot? No. If God was not at work through the ordinary means of a beautiful queen or a dinner invitation, then the book of Esther would have ended with the annihilation of God's chosen people. If God was not at work in the everyday moments of life thousands of years ago, then you and I have no hope for salvation now. There's good news: God was at work then and He is at work now in the normal rhythms of our lives!

Esther reminds us a bit of Moses and other Old Testament deliverers. She was far from perfect, as she compromised and concealed her identity. Moses doubted the wisdom of God that called him to be the guy who would be powerfully used by God to deliver God's the Israelites from slavery. He was an everyday man, nothing extraordinary, and yet God chose to work through him in supernatural ways.

What is God doing through everyday Esther? Oh, nothing more than rescuing and redeeming the lives of His people! There in Susa, God is keeping His covenant promises. He is being faithful to the unfaithful and doing so through normal means. He is working out the Joseph story all over again.

As for you, you meant evil against me, but God meant it for good, to bring it about that many people should be kept alive, as they are today.

Genesis 50:20

Longing For The Extraordinary

Christianity in our day lusts for spectacular glory, seeking it under every rock. But what if our walks with Christ are just average? What if the spectacular (as we define it) avoids us like the plague? Are we to think we are a *lesser* kind of follower of Christ? What if our Christian life is ordinary? The book of Esther is a breath of fresh air for ordinary Christians.

Believers often long for and demand a Red Sea experience that confirms God's faithfulness. When there is no Rea Sea we begin to think something is wrong, that God is no longer at with us. What often follows is an assault on God's character and questions begin to be asked: *Where is God? Why don't we see more of His power?* Yes, God's power might be revealed in the Red Sea moments but, His power is also revealed in the everyday, mundane rhythms of life. In either case, God is powerfully at work as He continues His redemptive purposes!

I find this incredibly encouraging. I am an everyday guy, an everyday pastor, seeking to care for an everyday church. Nothing supernaturally spectacular about any of it and yet so absolutely spectacular! Don't miss the miracle of God performing His redeeming work through us in the everyday rhythms of life. Most of us are not called to be used by God to split a sea in two; most of us are called to go to work, live in a neighborhood, and to faithfully serve Christ in our churches as we go about our ordinary lives. And, as we do, why not do what Esther did and toss out a dinner invitation and see what God might be up to?

After all, who of us has a salvation that is "natural?" There is no such salvation! When God breathes new life into an individual, that person has been raised from death to life through no personal effort of their own. If we are not paying attention, we might just miss the glory of it all!

I missed it in Esther for years. Have you noticed we tend to drift toward the fiery furnaces, the writing on a wall, and the healed blind man more than we do Esther's simple invitation to a dinner? Ask yourself: are you drawn to Paul's Damascus road while giving little thought to Simeon? Simeon is that *insignificant* guy found in Luke 2. The question is not intended to be corrective. It is asked only to help us realize how we are drawn to the supernatural and yawn at what seems to be the everyday stuff of life. However, it is in the everyday stuff that our lives are lived. In those moments, God is often working His miraculous through the means of ordinary routines.[65]

Have you wondered: "Where is the hand of God today? Why don't we see more of what we see in the book of Acts?" I believe that what we see in both Acts and Esther are for today. Acts and Esther are not at odds with each other. God certainly could have revealed Himself in Esther like He did in in the life of Paul. We need the God who shuts the mouths of lions found in Daniel and we need the simplicity of a dinner invitation that we see in Esther. The glory of God is displayed in both!

We like to put God in our nice, neat little boxes. We think, "*this* is how God should work." For this facet of His nature, we can all be grateful: He is bigger than our boxes! God is revealed in Esther by working through an ordinary person and using His ordinary grace to accomplish an extraordinary salvation! Do you see it in Esther? While we long for the extraordinary, we easily miss the ordinary means of God's grace. We unintentionally belittle ordinary grace and ordinary testimonies, preferring what we think of as radical grace. The unintended result is a diminishing amazement in the grace of God. All grace is radical grace! Ordinary grace is glorious grace! When the Holy God extends salvation to wretched sinners through ordinary means, it is always extraordinary and worthy of our worship!

---

[65] To study this topic further, I recommend Michael Horton's excellent book titled: Ordinary: Sustainable Faith in a Radical, Restless World

I can hear people say, "ordinary is just so, ordinary." Imagine the book titled: "My Average Life Now." Line up and get yourself a signed copy! We don't like ordinary and average is just average. Here are some examples of how we undermine the beauty of the ordinary:

- Longing for dynamic times of prayer, we become bored with the everyday routine of prayer.
- Listening to the powerful stories from the visiting missionary, we think about our shallow, non-adventurous life. It's just average Christianity, following Christ in the suburbs.
- Hungry for the supernatural, we belittle the "non-spectacular" gifts of the Spirit.
- Wanting the high powered, vibrant church, we minimize God's active grace in the faithful church that plods along.[66]
- Jealous for a more exciting testimony, we embellish ours or think it to be too boring to be shared.[67]

The glory of the Esther story is how she serves the Lord's purpose without Moses's staff or David's sling shot. Indeed, all she has to work with is a dinner invitation and her God! Rest assured, God is at work in your life, even in the mundane. He is working; He is saving. He is Sovereign and we are responsible. Moses needed to speak; David needed to sling the rock; Esther needed to roll up her sleeves and fight for her people by inviting the king to dinner. Gloriously unspectacular!

How great is our God! Esther is extraordinary in its ordinariness. The story reminds us of Jesus in many ways. Yes, Jesus certainly did perform many miracles. But Jesus came in a way we might not expect. The Almighty God came in a surprisingly ordinary human way. Actually, He came the same way we all did, as a baby! Imagine: God Himself not only took on human flesh but the flesh of a baby, birthed by a human mom in the dark corner of a manger in insignificant Bethlehem. He came in the weakness of humanity, not like we might expect. While it was indeed miraculous, He chose to

---

[66] http://metrolife.org/sermons/sermon/2015-02-01/iplod

[67] See: http://timmerwin.com/2015/04/to-all-those-with-a-boring-testimony/

come to us through ordinary means. No parade heralded His entrance, no kingly glories accompanied His arrival. He arrived as a common human baby.

So Esther approached the king and Ahasuerus spared her life and said to her,

"What is it, Queen Esther? What is your request? It shall be given you, even to the half of my kingdom." And Esther said, "If it please the king, let the king and Haman come today to a feast that I have prepared for the king."

Esther 5:3-4

The impulsive king offers her half of his kingdom! Nothing in the Esther story has prepared us for this kind of response. Persian law forbade this intrusion in the king's court. As the time is drawing near for Esther to reveal her Jewish heritage, we read and wonder, what will happen? Esther knew her life was on the line. But God was at work. What will Esther do with such a generous proposition on the table? She could easily save herself and let God's people fend for themselves. Maybe she should take him up on his offer! Esther replies, "come to a feast..." The king and Haman agree to join her at this feast, followed by another feast. I chuckle at the surprisingly human means that God used to orchestrate the deliverance of His people. Where is the big miraculous moment in the book of Esther? If a dinner isn't flashy enough for us, then it is nowhere to be found; Esther is just an everyday woman providing an everyday feast, fit for a king and his second in command.

On two occasions the king offered a blank check to Esther: "Even to the half of my kingdom it shall be fulfilled" (5:3, 7:2). However, it was not going to be quite that simple. You see, Ahasuerus had decreed something and Esther wanted that edict reversed. Reversing edicts in that ancient culture was impossible. They were binding, sealed with the king's ring.

Mordecai's enemy was seemingly winning. All was moving forward rather nicely according to Haman's plan. So much so that Esther chapter five ended with Haman rejoicing at the demise of his enemy. Mordecai and God's people were soon to be annihilated and Haman could go on living his life without the likes of Mordecai and friends. The dark storm clouds had set in and the enemy was winning. God's people were defeated. Here we see another foreshadowing of the Gospel.

Where there seemed to be no hope for God's people, God was orchestrating their deliverance. That is the story of Esther and it is the story of the entire Bible. It's the story of the cross and it is the story of every genuine follower of Christ. At the cross, Christ brought hope to the hopeless! In Jesus, we who faced a certain death were brought to life in Christ.

Haman is found rejoicing at the demise of God's people; the gallows have been constructed and the celebrations to follow have been set. Satan also rejoiced too early at the apparent demise of Jesus on the cross. Humanly speaking, it appeared as if God's plan of deliverance had failed on that hill called Calvary. The Son of God had died! Utter despair crushed His disciples. All their hopes were smashed as He was wrapped and placed in the tomb. Christ now dead, our enemy had delivered the final death blow. God was defeated and His people were without hope. However, just as God ushered in a reversal for His people living in Susa, He has brought a reversal to you and me. Jesus Christ rose from the grave! The cross and the empty tomb exclaims to us that He has accomplished, once again, the salvation of His people. The cross, rather than being the greatest moment of defeat, is history's greatest victory! Those with no hope now have hope in Christ Jesus! Sin, death, and Satan himself were defeated; we are now made alive in Christ Jesus!

Reflections:

- How has God worked in your life through everyday, ordinary means?

- How does God's activity in the ordinary encourage your faith for God to move in the mundane rhythms of life?

Chapter 9: **Turning Everyday People Into gods**

"Fear" in the biblical sense...includes being afraid of someone, but it extends to holding someone in awe, being controlled or mastered by people, worshipping other people, putting your trust in people, or needing people."

Edward T. Welch,
*When People Are Big and God is Small:
Overcoming Peer Pressure, Codependency, and the Fear of Man*

And Haman went out that day joyful and glad of heart. But when Haman saw Mordecai in the king's gate, that he neither rose nor trembled before him, he was filled with wrath against Mordecai. Nevertheless, Haman restrained himself and went home, and he sent and brought his friends and his wife Zeresh. And Haman recounted to them the splendor of his riches, the number of his sons, all the promotions with which the king had honored him, and how he had advanced him above the officials and the servants of the king. Then Haman said, "Even Queen Esther let no one but me come with the king to the feast she prepared. And tomorrow also I am invited by her together with the king. **Yet all this is worth nothing to me, so long as I see Mordecai the Jew sitting at the king's gate.***" Then his wife Zeresh and all his friends said to him, "Let a gallows fifty cubits high be made, and in the morning tell the king to have Mordecai hanged upon it. Then go joyfully with the king to the feast." This idea pleased Haman, and he had the gallows made.*

Esther 5:9-14

Idolatry

While the Esther story is "ordinary," Haman thought of himself as extraordinary. He wrongfully assumed that he had become a somebody who had deservedly reached the apex. Speaking to his wife, he boasted *"Even Queen Esther let no one but me come with the king...."* However, while Haman had been given an enormous amount of power, his life spun out of control. The promotion that should have made his life easier became the very reason he fell into a downward spiral. All this, simply because of his inability to control one man. Ironically, the lack of homage from this one man, the inability to *rule* him, became the catalyst that *ruled* Haman.

Ask yourself: *What was ruling Haman's actions? What did he crave? What determined his next move? How far was Haman willing to go to get what he wanted? If Mordecai would have bowed his knee, how would the Esther story have ended?* Indeed, Mordecai had become a twisted sort of god to Haman. Mordecai's determined inaction ruled Hamaan's actions. This unacceptable posture became the fertile soil for Haman's impatience and anger to grow. His idol refused to give him what he craved the most, Mordecai's worship. Interestingly, Haman's behavior was being determined by the actions of his enemy. This is the folly of idolatry! Idols are not just an ancient pagan issue, they are an issue for today and an issue for believers. When the apostle John penned his first letter he addressed the believers, not the unbelievers, when he wrote, "Children, keep yourself from idols."[68] Haman's longing for honor eventually drove him to his grave. Idols are cruel taskmasters! As the desire for someone or something takes over, desire for what honors God takes a back seat. Simply put, an idol is anything that takes the place of God.

When I read this chapter in Esther, I want to speak to the Haman in me and say: *Tim, there is a better way. God resists the proud but He gives grace to the humble. Humble yourself!* The road of humble repentance would have brought this story to a radically different ending for Haman. I need to be reminded of this truth because in many ways I am Haman. We are either worshiping God or we are serving someone or something else. Contrary to what we

---

[68] 1 John 5:21

might think, we do not remain indifferent. Our actions give us away, revealing who or what we serve. Christians and non-Christians alike, we all have this impulse to turn everyday people and things into gods. "Not me," I can hear you say as you consider skipping this chapter. I invite you to stick around; this brief chapter might offer you freedoms not yet realized.

When People Are gods

We pick up our story as Haman walked home after the private dinner, glad of heart and drunk on his own new found prestige. After all, he kept company with the king and queen! Haman loved who he had become but one thing was missing. He invited the neighbors to his house so that he might *"recount to them the splendor of his riches, the number of his sons, all the promotions with which the king had honored him, and how he had advanced him above the officials and servants of the king...."* On and on it went. Haman blabbered to his friends about his good fortune and the important man he had become in the powerful kingdom. One might have expected Haman to launch into how lucky his friends were just to know him! This narcissism is what ruled his heart. His new position in the kingdom demanded honor and respect. For the most part, his subjects played along. Haman was worshiped. He loved his prominence and wanted everyone to know it. However, 99% participation wasn't enough, he lusted for more, especially from the one man in the kingdom that refused to give him what he wanted. His arch enemy, Mordecai.

Before we march too far into our self-righteous hypocrisy, we would do well to note how much we make of our reputation and people's opinions of us. Make no mistake about it: opinions matter far too much to us and when opinions take on an elevated role, they begin to rule us. Actions once done for the glory of God, are now performed for the glory of me. We like being liked and we want people to be impressed by who we are and the company we keep. Behold our god! This rulership is a crummy master. When we make others' opinions to be what we live for, we have essentially turned people into a god. Man's opinions, not God's, begins to determine how we might act or speak. Ask yourself: *How much do people's opinions and approval determine what you do and how you do it?* Still not convinced?

A couple started to date when a shift took place in the relationship. While they might never admit it, the couple started worshiping each other. This idolatry can lead to temptations and the compromising of morals, ending in heartbreak and sometimes unwanted pregnancy. Without the covenant of marriage between them, the man sinfully denies responsibility and idolizes his comfort while the woman, still worshipping her boyfriend's acceptance and attention, seeks an abortion.

Perhaps that example doesn't intersect your life. Allow me to touch on other everyday illustrations of exalting human opinions to god-like status. In each of these examples consider: who or what is the ruling opinion affecting the decisions?

- Not wanting to appear stupid, he cheated on his exams throughout high school.

- Longing to be the life of the party, she drank excessively although she hated the taste of alcohol.

- Wanting a promotion at work and needing the extra money to pay the bills, he regularly changed who he was when the boss was nearby. He became kinder, laughed at the boss' crude jokes, and willingly participated in questionable activities that the boss asked of him.

- She raised her hands and sang loudly at her church because she knew that the *cute guy* who seemed serious about the Lord was sitting a few rows behind her.

- He answered his dad's question, not out of honesty and conviction, but with the answer he knew his dad wanted to hear.

- A dad berates and demands respect from the children when they do not immediately respond to his request.

- A mom invited a friend and her kids over to the house for the afternoon. The friend's children were very well-behaved, while her children became unruly. Afraid of her friend's opinion of her, she took her own children behind a closed door and scolded them harshly. This reprimand did not come from a desire to train them. She was driven by the desire to be thought of as a "good parent." A mom whose children respect her.

- She was recognized publicly for serving in the church you attend. You begin to think: *I have never been publicly recognized for the serving I have done...Why do I bother?* Rather than rejoicing with her, your heart grew in bitterness.

- He set out to write a book. What will people think? Will it be accepted, criticized, or ignored altogether? Yep, that one is for me. What you're reading is that book and writing it has been instrumental as God has been helping me to put to death this idolatry of others' opinions.

Anger, despair, anxiety, cravings, and many more examples could be given in how we are ruled, not by God's opinion, but man's. Our longing for the approval of man is so great that we have all done things we would not have dreamed of doing for reasons we do not wish to acknowledge.

We need to recognize that this elevation of people is a diminishing of God. Our problem is a God problem as we have misplaced our worship and who it is we live for. Will we live for the approval of people or of God? Who will we worship, God or man? Our hearts are swayed by the approval of others rather than the approval of God. Man, not God, rules our hearts. What is the solution to our madness? We need to behold the glory of our God. When people are made to be big, God becomes small.[69] I have found that studying the attributes of God can be a useful remedy to our dilemma. Exploring and studying His wide ranging attributes, is a strong antidote to the poison idols introduce. When God is small, we need to read our Bibles asking: "Who is God in this text?" "What attributes of

---

[69] For further development of this topic I recommend Ed Welch's book: When People Are Big And God Is Small.

God are being revealed in this passage of Scripture?" That is, after all, the reason God's Word exists. Consider the attributes of God that we have been exploring thus far in Esther. He is *the* Sovereign King whose reign is steadfast, patient, faithful and all-powerful. He is the Covenant Keeper who will rescue His people. He is the Savior who came to earth to be our Redeemer and Mediator. He is the Groom who doesn't forsake His bride. He is the Sacrifice who restored our relationship with the Father and atoned for our sins.[70] Behold your God!

This craving, desire, or lust of our hearts that longs for approval turns quickly into the worship of others. If the people we hold in high esteem are impressed and lend us time and attention, we experience a high. Interestingly, anxiety and complaining suddenly disappear. Like Haman, we recount all the good fortunes in our lives. But, if those people-turned-gods do not return our flattery, recognize our position, ignore our sacrifice, or neglect our service, then we experience discouragement and bitterness. Why? Because something other than God is ruling our hearts.

Imagine with me as Haman's honor was slighted by a nobody. Who was Mordecai to Haman? Why did Mordecai's opinion matter to Haman? Indeed, what a ridiculous overreaction by Haman! Having been disrespected by one man, he sought not only the death of Mordecai but also he thirsted for the death of *all* the Jews. *"Death to him and all those like him."* The book of James chimes in on what's going on in Haman's heart.

What causes quarrels and what causes fights among you? Is it not this, that your passions are at war within you? You desire and do not have, so you murder. You covet and cannot obtain, so you fight and quarrel.

James 4:1-2

How about you? Can you crawl into Haman's response and James 4? I am enjoying the effort it is taking to pen this book. And

---

[70] Consider doing a study on the attributes of God with one of these excellent books: A.W. Tozer, The Attributes of God Volume 1 and 2; A.W. Pink, The Attributes of God; Paul Tripp, Awe; John Piper, The Pleasures of God; R.C. Sproul, The Holiness of God; Jen Wilken, None Like Him.

yet, I don't think I like it at all. Why? Because putting pen to paper is convicting! I don't like admitting there is something of a Haman in me, desiring to rule me! However, we must consistently return to the good news: Christ came to set us free from our Haman-like moments!

Haman's idol, the approval and recognition of one man, ruled his actions. As Mordecai refused to feed that idol Haman instantly shifted from elation to anger. How about we have a moment of honest reflection? What brings you to that place where anger flashes in your eyes most quickly?

For am I now seeking the approval of man, or of God? Or am I trying to please man? If I were still trying to please man, I would not be a servant of Christ.

Galatians 1:10

The fear of man lays a snare, but whoever trusts in the LORD is safe.

Proverbs 29:25

Who Or What Is Your Mordecai?

While we might pretend not to care, we desire our *Mordecai* to honor us. We worship being worshiped. As long as Haman was recognized with private feasts and promotions, all went well. But when a single Jewish man did not bow to him, Haman's kingdom fell apart. Where do you see this dynamic taking place in your life? Ask yourself: am I a slave to people's opinions? Does the approval of man control me like the strings of a puppet? While we desire to control people so they might give us the recognition we think we deserve, the reality is we are being controlled not unlike Haman.

I find that pastoring is a regular opportunity to seek to kill this worship of man. As I mentioned, I pastor Trinity Community Church. It is a great church, though not without its challenges. But I love it! Quite a few years ago we went through some unexpected challenges. As with much of the country, our local economy began to decline. Our church is located on the space coast of Florida. When the government closed down the space shuttle program in 2011, the church began to shrink. Locals from Titusville often describe where they are from by saying something like, "I live where they *used* to launch the space shuttle." My wife asked me one day how I was doing with the coming changes. Little did I know that soon I was going to be pastoring a church in a *used to* city. I knew the *right* answers: I even thought I believed them! I told her that I was not concerned, appearing as if I was the great man of faith. "It will be alright," I said. "If the church shrinks down to a small number, I will be okay with that." Then it did just that and I soon found out that I was not "okay with that." People lost their homes and employment. Some had to leave to find work in another city or state. There were also those who desired to make a change and attend other local churches and the church shrunk more. Additionally, we moved forward with an overdue church plant an hour south of our location, and the church continued to shrink.

All this began to reveal that I was not "okay" like I had told my wife. In the process of leading a shrinking church, I became aware of how much I was driven by people's opinions. Sadly, the number of people in the room began to rule me, becoming my identity. I wanted to be respected and this want became a god; I had an identity problem and a significant desire for man's approval, a dangerous place for pastors that often drives them to compromise convictions and water down God's Word. God, in His kindness, began to reveal to me just how much my identity was wrapped up in having a full building, and what I believed others thought was a *respectable* size. My identity as a pastor was being tested and I had lost my way! Rather than finding my identity in Christ, my identity was in what I perceived were people's opinions of me.

The Lord is a jealous God. He died so that we might find our identity to be found in Christ. How sad it is to reflect back and see just how ruled I was by people's opinions and how much I was neglecting who I was in Christ. Though those days were extremely difficult, as many friends had to pack up their families and move from the area, I am grateful for the trials. God in His patience and kindness used this season to expose idols in me that I didn't know existed. He is a caring God who is committed to our sanctification!

Back To The Counselor's Couch

What Haman told his wife and friends was a window into his heart. He recounted and said, *"Look all that I have, look at what I have become, and look at how important I am by the company I keep."* Yet, none of that retained any sort of value as long as Haman's god, Mordecai, was alive.

How will his friends bring wisdom to Haman? How will they lovingly address his heart? Will they tell him what he wants to hear or what he needs to hear? Sadly, the counsel they offer is also rooted in man's approval. Rather than helping Haman destroy the idol, they feed it! Caution: you do not want the friends around you to turn you into their god. This situation will cause them to do little more than take up your offense and agree with you. That is what Haman's wife and friends did, all the way to his death!

"Build the gallows and hang Mordecai on them," they said. Why? Because Mordecai was not giving you what you wanted, what you thought you deserved. He dissed you publicly so make a public example of him! This vengeful attitude is not the counsel that Haman needed to hear. How about a different approach? Haman, what was going on in your heart that you were so consumed by Mordecai's worship of you? What was ruling you? What did you so desperately desire that you were not getting? Why such anger, joy, and anger again?

Haman enjoyed their sympathy. But sympathy was not what was necessary. You and I need friends who will love us enough to speak the healing words of grace and truth. The gallows were constructed ridiculously tall (Fifty Cubits) for all to see. Fifty cubits tall is the equivalent to seventy-five feet! Since Mordecai would not honor Haman publicly, Haman was determined to dishonor him publicly by humiliating him in death from an inordinate height. As we consider Haman, we are reminded that Christ was lifted high, dishonored, and publicly humiliated on Calvary's hill.

Because of the cross of Christ, we can now find our identity in the Savior and not in the approval of man. Our hope is not in the fickle opinions of people; it is in the settled opinions of God through Christ's sacrifice. We are sons or daughters of the living God. He has not only saved us, but He also adopted us! He is our heavenly Father! We are approved by Him, not because we have behaved well enough, but because Jesus earned the Father's approval for us. We belong to God! His opinions of us are unchanging, rooted in the finished work of Jesus Christ on the cross!

Behold your gods and then, behold your God!

Reflections:

- Prayerfully consider: *What causes quarrels and what causes fights among you? Is it not this, that your passions are at war within you? You desire and do not have, so you murder. You covet and cannot obtain, so you fight and quarrel. James 4:1-2*

- What moves you from joy to anger in an instant? What are you not receiving that you are willing to make light of the cross and sin your way into obtaining for yourself?

Chapter 10: A Sleepless Night Brings A Daytime Nightmare

"Life is but a Weaving"

My life is but a weaving
Between my God and me.
I cannot choose the colors
He weaveth steadily.

Oft' times He weaveth sorrow;
And I in foolish pride
Forget He sees the upper
And I the underside.

Not 'til the loom is silent
And the shuttles cease to fly
Will God unroll the canvas
And reveal the reason why.

The dark threads are as needful
In the weaver's skillful hand
As the threads of gold and silver
In the pattern He has planned

He knows, He loves, He cares;
Nothing this truth can dim.
He gives the very best to those
Who leave the choice to Him.

Corrie ten Boom

On that night the king could not sleep. And he gave orders to bring the book of memorable deeds, the chronicles, and they were read before the king. And it was found written how Mordecai had told about Bigthana and Teresh, two of the king's eunuchs, who guarded the threshold, and who had sought to lay hands on King Ahasuerus. And the king said, "What honor or distinction has been bestowed on Mordecai for this?" The king's young men who attended him said, "Nothing has been done for him."

Esther 6:1-3

Checkmate

The tapestry, in the hands of the weaver, is a work of art from the front side and mess from the back. "Of't times He weaveth sorrow; / And I in foolish pride / Forget He sees the upper / And I the underside." Here in Esther 6, we are given the benefit of seeing the upper and underside of the tapestry.

While God remains unmentioned by both the author and the characters found in Esther, He was at work in the sleepless night of the king. The chess match continued. Haman made his move and confidently determined in his mind that the King of the Jews was in check. "Not so fast," came the reply. After a night of sleeplessness, the King of all kings proclaimed "Check...mate!"[71]

In the kindness of God, we have a record of God's faithfulness, a written account of how God interacted with His creation through the ages. God increasingly makes Himself known on the written pages of His Word. Therefore, we would do well to read His book seeking to better know God, who He is and all that He has done. We tend to read the Bible with ourselves in the forefront and God in the background. While in reality, God is in the forefront and we're in the background. Our prideful hearts might not like to hear that; we like to be the center of attention. But God's Word exists to reveal our faithful God.

---

[71] Credit to John McArthur for this analogy. https://www.gty.org

113

Who is God in Esther? What attributes has God revealed to us in this little book? Thus far, we might say "God has been invisible," in Esther. This apparent absence has led us to question, where is God? The two questions: who is God and where is God are not dissimilar. While God is not mentioned, He is the God who *is* there! As we begin to see the God who *is* there, we are then postured to consider who He is. He is unmentioned, yet He is the God who is at work on that sleepless night which makes the invisible God visible.

As decadence moves from the outer fringes to the normal center of life, Christians begin to get nervous. *"Where is God in America? Where is God in our government, schools, and churches? Where are we headed?"* People and churches begin to get desperate thinking that something isn't working so they shift to *try* something else. Some turn to politics, others to picketing and boycotting. Some look to education and still others to any number of false saviors. Esther's story helps us to turn our gaze away from these incompetent saviors and direct us to our sovereign King. While we ought to participate in our political processes, engage on policies and encourage education, none of these are the hope of the world. Esther exists to point us to the God who is! When God is not named in Susa or wherever you live, we are to read Esther and realize that God has never ceased being God! When society refuses to recognize Him and when culture seeks to dismiss Him, He is still the King who rules from heaven's throne! Esther shows us that He continues His work, redeeming lives for His glory alone!

If there is one thing we should come away with when reading our bibles, it is this: God is at work, He is on high, and He will accomplish the redemption of His people, all for His glory. God will have a people then and now! No government or king or educator or culture has the power to thwart the mighty saving hand of God. That is the book of Esther! How can we be certain of this? Look no further than yourself. Christian, you and I are living proof that God is still at work, redeeming lives for His glory!

While Mordecai, Esther, and the other Jews found themselves in Susa because their ancestors had been unfaithful, God makes Himself known to us as our faithful God. While king Ahasuerus was an uncommitted husband that cast Vashti aside, our God is a faithful

King and loyal Groom who never forsakes His bride. Therefore, God was at work in the stillness of the night. The king did not sleep because *the* King never sleeps or slumbers.

I lift up my eyes to the hills. From where does my help come?
My help comes from the LORD, who made heaven and earth.
He will not let your foot be moved; he who keeps you will not slumber.
Behold, he who keeps Israel will neither slumber nor sleep.

Psalms 121:1-4

God's Care Through The Night

...do not be anxious about anything, but in everything by prayer and supplication with thanksgiving let your requests be made known to God. And the peace of God, which surpasses all understanding, will guard your hearts and your minds in Christ Jesus.

Philippians 4:7-8

We can "be anxious for nothing" because we know that God is at work while we sleep. What kept the king awake at night? We don't know. Perhaps we ought to think of it as yet another extraordinarily ordinary moment in Esther. We are led to understand that the king remained awake because God had not finished the story. If the king had slept well on that night, Mordecai would have been hanged from the gallows and all the Jews would have died. While Esther held a small feast for three, seeking to build enough courage to appeal to the king and while the Jews fasted, the reality was the circumstances were already beyond their control. When there was no hope and Esther, Mordecai and Haman slept, the king remained awake because *the* King was at work. And when the enemy of your soul aligned himself against you, God never slept!

You may have grown up in a home where God's name was never mentioned except when cursing. Perhaps you were what some call an *accident* or maybe you did not grow up in a loving family. Some who are reading this book were physically harmed. Others were neglected altogether. These unimaginable horrors, as painful and

115

difficult as they are, were no match for the Sovereign King who continued to work out your salvation, even while you slept!

Behold your God!

A Psalm of David.

The LORD is my shepherd; I shall not want.
He makes me lie down in green pastures.
He leads me beside still waters. He restores my soul.
He leads me in paths of righteousness for his name's sake.
Even though I walk through the valley of the shadow of death,
I will fear no evil, for you are with me;
your rod and your staff, they comfort me.

You prepare a table before me in the presence of my enemies;
you anoint my head with oil; my cup overflows.
Surely goodness and mercy shall follow me all the days of my life,
and I shall dwell in the house of the LORD forever.

Psalm 23

I like to meditate on this astonishing Psalm. Sometimes I get overly familiar with it, leading me to disregard its glories too easily. Consider the range it covers. Not only is God found to be leading us to green pastures and still waters (a picture of rest and peace) but He is also found to be preparing a table in the presence of my enemies (a picture of unwavering steadiness in the face of battle). It is good for my soul to consider the opening verse by emphasizing each word.

- The <u>LORD</u> is my Shepherd. Who shepherds you? The Lord does! The God of the universe, the Lord who created it all, the One who left the comforts of heaven and came to die for you. The Lord who rose and ascended is now seated at the right hand of the Father, He is the One who Shepherds you! He sent His Spirit who now lives in you as your Advocate and Helper. Yes, He is The LORD in every sense of the word. The LORD is my Shepherd, indeed!

116

- The Lord **IS** my Shepherd. Yes, He has been my Shepherd (past) and He will be my Shepherd (future), but He *is* my Shepherd (presently). I trust you are immensely comforted by those words, "the Lord is my Shepherd." As death loomed over the Jews they anxiously slept while the King shepherded His people. Amazingly, He is shepherding you at this very moment!

- The Lord is **MY** Shepherd. Astoundingly, the Creator of the universe is not distant. His care for you and me is personal. How great is our God? As Shepherd, He leaves the ninety-nine to go after the one lost sheep. There was a time when that lost sheep was you and me. Praise Him, the Lord's care for you is personal!

- The Lord is my **SHEPHERD**. This means that God protects, cares for, feeds, and personally guides you. How amazing is this opening line of Psalms 23? On that sleepless night in Susa, God was busy shepherding His people.

I am the good shepherd. The good shepherd lays down his life for the sheep. He who is a hired hand and not a shepherd, who does not own the sheep, sees the wolf coming and leaves the sheep and flees, and the wolf snatches them and scatters them. He flees because he is a hired hand and cares nothing for the sheep. I am the good shepherd. I know my own and my own know me, just as the Father knows me and I know the Father; and I lay down my life for the sheep.

John 10:11-15

Haman's Big Day

Remember, Haman had become a somebody. He was on the fast track to success as he attended the private banquet of the queen! There was one nagging thorn that remained and that too was soon to be handled. His life, he thought, had turned for the better. Who wouldn't want to be him? He had arrived at where many of us are desperately trying to go. If only Haman would only repented. Imagine how this story might have then unfolded.

117

And the king said, "Who is in the court?" Now Haman had just entered the outer court of the king's palace to speak to the king about having Mordecai hanged on the gallows that he had prepared for him. And the king's young men told him, "Haman is there, standing in the court." And the king said, "Let him come in."

As the king remained sleepless, Haman awoke early in the morning with anticipation. He was refreshed and ready to go. This was the day he had been waiting for! The paint was still drying on the newly constructed gallows. Haman was soon going to be feasting and enjoying another private meal with the royal couple and his nemesis was to be hanged from the gallows in a public shaming before the day ended! His life, he believed, could not be going better. Nothing had prepared him for what came next:

*So Haman came in, and the king said to him, "What should be done to the man whom the king delights to honor?" And Haman said to himself, "Whom would the king delight to honor more than me?" And Haman said to the king, "For the man whom the king delights to honor, let royal robes be brought, which the king has worn, and the horse that the king has ridden, and on whose head a royal crown is set. And let the robes and the horse be handed over to one of the king's most noble officials. Let them dress the man whom the king delights to honor, and let them lead him on the horse through the square of the city, proclaiming before him: 'Thus shall it be done to the man whom the king delights to honor.'" Then the king said to Haman, "Hurry; take the robes and the horse, as you have said, **and do so to Mordecai the Jew**, who sits at the king's gate. Leave out nothing that you have mentioned."*

Esther 6:5-10

Having had the opportunity to read the chronicles through the night, the king decided to reward the man who had previously saved his life. The king asked Haman, *"How should I honor the man....?"* Haman jumped at the bait thinking, *"of course the king desires to honor me!"* Hook, line, and sinker! Haman was all in on the plan to honor a man like *himself!* He had perhaps spent some sleepless nights of his own mulling over this very question. *"So glad you asked, it just so happens I have been wondering the same thing... oh, great king!"* Haman's reply was exactly what he himself wanted: *"Throw that man a parade worthy of royalty, march him through the streets and publicly esteem him!"* His suggestion of the royal robe and crown was an honoring worthy of a king.

The king thought this was a good plan and replied, *"yes, good, go do that for* **Mordecai***!"*

I try to imagine the horror of this moment. Heart pounding and veins pulsing, Haman wondered if his ears had somehow tricked him. *Did the king just order me to publicly honor the man who has been publicly dishonoring me?* The best day of Haman's life had just become the worst day of his life. Haman was a living parable of the great proverb,

Pride goes before destruction, and a haughty spirit before a fall.

Proverbs 16:18

Tables Turned

So Haman took the robes and the horse, and he dressed Mordecai and led him through the square of the city, proclaiming before him, "Thus shall it be done to the man whom the king delights to honor."

Esther 6:11

Imagine as Haman dressed Mordecai in those royal robes worthy of a king. The last time the book referenced Mordecai's apparel, he was clothed in sackcloth and ashes! The tables had turned. The man who refused to lower himself to Haman was lifted atop of the king's horse by the hand of his enemy. The sleepless night of the king proved to be the hinge moment in the story of Esther as the tables turned for both Haman and Mordecai. Neither one of them saw this unimaginable day coming!

The tables continued to turn as Haman returned home to his wife and friends, completely humiliated. Certainly, they will be a source of comfort to his wounded soul. They were, after all, the ones who suggested the scheme, complete with gallows. Zeresh and friends, however, now held a different opinion of things. *"If Mordecai is a Jew,"* they said, *"then you will surely fall before him."* Where was this counsel a day ago? Not only had Haman's schemes turned and not only did the king's plans begin to shift, but his own wife and closest friends had also turned against him. Those friends had suddenly become theologically astute! Iain Duguid asks,

> *What about us? Are we as quick to spot the hand of God at work as were Haman's wife and friends, or as slow to believe as his covenant people? We ought to have an unshakable confidence that, despite all appearances, God will act to bring about the salvation of his people. This confidence should drive us to act boldly in faith. Yet the reality is that we easily get thrown by circumstances that seem to be conspiring to bring about our downfall. Surprising as it may seem, we can learn a more godly response from Zeresh and Haman's friends.* [72]

While the author of Esther continues to omit any mention of God, even the dialogue of Haman's wife and friends carries us along to see the faithfulness of our King. These individuals who encouraged Mordecai's death seemingly became perceptive to the redemptive storyline. It is an unmistakable glory. God is not named but we have come to see His hand on every page. The sleepless night of the king was no more coincidence than Esther's beauty and Mordecai's hearing of the assassination plot. God is *the* King who is orchestrating His plan in Susa!

---

[72]Iain M. Duguid. Esther & Ruth (Reformed Expository Commentary). Kindle Edition.

As the tables turned, we might expect to find Haman brought to his knees in humility. However, having been publicly humiliated and receiving no comfort from his wife and friends, the chapter ends with Haman heading off to another feast with the king and queen. In Haman's mind, things could not get worse. But before we get to that, consider Esther's Gospel.

The King's Parade

Mordecai's parade reminds us of another parade. King Jesus arrived many years later riding into Jerusalem on a donkey as the gathered crowd threw its cloaks on the ground before Him. It was a rare moment of honor in the life of Christ. Days later he was again paraded through the streets but this time he carried the cross in public humiliation. While Mordecai was clothed in the royal robes, Christ was disrobed and then clothed in His own blood.

The Jews were awaiting their impending death when the tables turned and Haman clothed Mordecai in royal garments. We too were awaiting our death when Christ saved us and clothed us in the royal robes of His righteousness! We, like Haman and Mordecai, never saw that day coming. The king proclaimed, "give Mordecai the royal crown to wear in the streets." Christ was given a crown of thorns, pressed into His brow. The honoring of Mordecai became the dishonoring of Haman. Ahasuerus commanded Haman to *"Proclaim it through the streets."* Years later, it was also proclaimed of Jesus by soldiers mockingly shouting: *"This is your King, Hail the King of the Jews!"* And, They crucified Him!

What an unexpected turn of the tables we see in Susa. The decree of death that hung over Mordecai turned into a parade in his honor. Likewise, we too had a decree hanging over us but because of the cross of Christ, we have been saved from the sentence of death.

One turn of the tables remains unmentioned. In history's greatest turn of events, Christ rose from the grave! The King has risen, behold your God! Now we await that future day when there will be one final parade of the King. He carried the cross in one parade but He will ride on a white horse in the next. Once mocked and humiliated, He will be clothed in splendor when He returns for His bride! On that day He will be rightly honored and we will joyfully fall before Him in the worship of *the* King!

Then I looked, and I heard around the throne and the living creatures and the elders the voice of many angels, numbering myriads of myriads and thousands of thousands, saying with a loud voice, "Worthy is the Lamb who was slain, to receive power and wealth and wisdom and might and honor and glory and blessing!"

And I heard every creature in heaven and on earth and under the earth and in the sea, and all that is in them, saying, "To him who sits on the throne and to the Lamb be blessing and honor and glory and might forever and ever!"

Revelation 5:11-13

Reflections:

- How have you come to see the seemingly random circumstances in your life's tapestry to be the hand of God?

- How did God turn the tables in your life to bring about your salvation?

Chapter 11: **Justice in Susa**

"My argument against God was that the universe seemed so cruel and unjust. But how had I got this idea of just and unjust? A man does not call a line crooked unless he has some idea of a straight line. What was I comparing this universe with when I called it unjust?"

C.S. Lewis, Mere Christianity

If I Have Found Favor

While they were yet talking with him, the king's eunuchs arrived and hurried to bring Haman to the feast that Esther had prepared. So the king and Haman went in to feast with Queen Esther. And on the second day, as they were drinking wine after the feast, the king again said to Esther, "What is your wish, Queen Esther? It shall be granted you. And what is your request? Even to the half of my kingdom, it shall be fulfilled. Then Queen Esther answered, "If I have found favor in your sight, O king, and if it please the king, let my life be granted me for my wish, and my people for my request.

Esther 6:14-7:3

While God remains unmentioned, He is at work in the sleepless night of the king bringing about the salvation of his people. Haman's day hadn't gone as planned before the eunuchs arrived, hurrying him to the queen's feast. Little did he know that they would also be hurrying him out from this same feast. Glad to have the earlier events of the day behind him, perhaps he cheered himself up by reminded himself of whose company he'd soon be keeping.

Once again the king asked Esther what she wished for, offering her up to half of his kingdom. Up to this point, neither

Haman nor the king knew that Esther was a Jew. Furthermore, Haman had no idea that the decree he had manipulated the king to issue was a death sentence against his Majesty's queen. *"So, go ahead, Esther,"* the king welcomed any and all requests from his queen. I imagine Haman had loosened up a bit from the humiliating events earlier that day. Having enjoyed the royal wine, he too wanted to know what Esther desired. Can you see him leaning forward from his chair, thinking *"yeah Esther, just what is it that you wish?"*

"If I have found favor...." Esther stammered, *"Let my life be granted for my wish and my people..."* Nothing had prepared Haman for what happened next.

...For we have been sold, I and my people, to be destroyed, to be killed, and to be annihilated. If we had been sold merely as slaves, men and women, I would have been silent, for our affliction is not to be compared with the loss to the king." Then King Ahasuerus said to Queen Esther, **"Who is he, and where is he, who has dared to do this?"** And Esther said, *"A foe and enemy! This wicked Haman!"* Then Haman was terrified before the king and the queen.

Esther 7:4-6

Remember, all these events were avoidable. Haman's pride led him to his ultimate demise. The utter destruction of God's people was what Haman wanted. Instead, self-destruction was what he received. 1 Peter 5:6 tells us to *Humble yourselves, therefore, under the mighty hand of God so that at the proper time he may exalt you, casting all your anxieties on him, because he cares for you.* Once again, James tells us that *God opposes the proud.* I don't want to be opposed by God yet it is quite amazing how easily proud comments or thoughts flow out of my heart and off my lips. We like to be right and we want everyone around us to recognize just how right we are. Consider a few questions to help evaluate our pride:

- Do you always feel the need to have the last word or to win the argument?

- Do you think your perspective is the right one and all other people just don't quite get it like you do?
- Do you wish that the people around you would think and act like you?
- Does conflict seem to follow you?
- Are you easily angered or quick to lose your patience?
- Are you a good listener?
- Do you prefer to be the one speaking?
- Are you immediately offended when someone is trying to help you see their perspective when it disagrees with yours?
- Do you find it difficult to admit where you *might* be wrong?
- Do the walls of defense quickly rise to justify your words or actions?
- Do you think: *how dare YOU to point out MY faults?*
- Consider, how much energy you have put into thinking about *yourself* as you review that last conflict with a co-worker.

Friends, we are full of pride! The good news is that James also tells us that God gives grace to the humble! Our prayer should be, *"God help me to increasingly receive grace by growing in humility."*

Haman was not simply defying the Jews; he had postured Himself against the God of the Jews. His actions were in direct opposition to God and the redemption of His people. Esther made her appeal to Ahasuerus but it was ultimately up to *the* King to providentially move the heart of the king.

The heart of man plans his way,
but the LORD establishes his steps.

Proverbs 16:9

Behold, the nations are like a drop from a bucket, and are accounted as the dust on the scales; behold, he takes up the coastlands like fine dust.

Isaiah 40:15

We can plan our words and make our appeals to the kings of this world, but God must move. Therefore, the shift in the king's heart was not due to Esther's eloquence or the delicious meal. To be sure, God can use anything but our hope for change is not found in our finely delivered speeches or our efforts of any sort; it is established in the mighty hand of God!

Esther did well to explain that, if her people were only to be sold as slaves, she would have remained silent but since her people were to be annihilated she must plead. Notice Esther invokes the same compilation of words (7:4) that Haman used in the original decree (Esther 3:13). For the second time on this day, the room began to spin and Haman couldn't believe his ears! The king was aghast by Esther's words as he demanded to know who had dared to initiate such a horrid thing. Her reply was biting: *"wicked Haman!"*

The king was now aware that the man he had vested with power and authority had used his position to plot the death of his queen and all of her people. Haman was terrified as the angry king Ahasuerus left the room.

And the king arose in his wrath from the wine-drinking and went into the palace garden, but Haman stayed to beg for his life from Queen Esther, for he saw that harm was determined against him by the king.

Esther 7:7

The Verdict

Remember, this king was renowned for his fits of rage. Haman had probably witnessed more than a few of his tirades. As soon as the king had left the room, Haman began to plead for his life from the woman who, moments before, pleaded for her life! In an absolute panic, Haman fell before Esther.

And the king returned from the palace garden to the place where they were drinking wine, as Haman was falling on the couch where Esther was. And the king said, "Will he even assault the queen in my presence, in my own house?" As the word left the mouth of the king, they covered Haman's face.

Esther 7:8

As the king returned, he found Haman falling on the couch where Esther was reclining. The king was immediately infuriated as Haman's action appeared to be an assault on the queen, in the king's palace no less. A cover was placed over Haman's face and one of the king's eunuchs informed the king that Haman's gallows stood ready. Those same gallows that had been prepared for Mordecai, the man honored by the king in the streets earlier that day! The story continues to advance at a rapid pace as everything prior has been building up to this moment.

And the king said, "Hang him on that." So they hanged Haman on the gallows that he had prepared for Mordecai. Then the wrath of the king abated....
On that day King Ahasuerus gave to Queen Esther the house of Haman, the enemy of the Jews. And Mordecai came before the king, for Esther had told what he was to her. And the king took off his signet ring, which he had taken from Haman, and gave it to Mordecai. And Esther set Mordecai over the house of Haman.

Esther 7:8-9; 8:1-2

The king's proclamation was swift, *"hang him on that."* Behold our gods and the downward spiral awaiting all who trust in them. God's word serves as a warning for us. Haman's god of recognition ruled him to the extent that we might say he gave his life to his god. While it might be easy to look at Haman and see the foolishness of his heart, Esther exists to help us to humbly look at our own lives and recognize that Christ died to save us from our foolishness. Are you placing your trust in other gods? How is it that we so easily identify the false gods in Haman, while struggling to see our own?

The investments can seemingly dwindle overnight. As they disappear, all hope vanishes with them. We begin to lose sleep, eating is no longer enjoyable, and we become increasingly irritable and short with the family. We thought we trusted God but the falling market reveals we have placed our trust in a false god, a false hope. Is your trust found in your husband or wife? *If he would lead our home better our family would be complete. If she would show me the respect I deserve we would finally get somewhere.* How many Christians have placed their hope in their pastor? As a pastor, I appreciate the respect that has been shown me but pastors are not the Savior! We must get our eyes off of man and focus them squarely on Jesus Christ! He is our only hope! Are you trusting in your own strength to mortify sin? Our hope in having victory over sin must be rooted in God! Good news, He is working to purify us and to make us more like Him! Is Jesus enough? Or, do we finally find hope when we have Jesus plus a good retirement account, a dream marriage, or the perfect career? Houses can fall; cars will rust; investments might dry up but the Lord is everlasting. Incline your heart towards Him! He is the source of your security, assurance, and joy.

That is why we have the story of Esther. Ultimately, Esther is more than the story of Esther. It is the story of God. He is faithfully involved in the lives of His people, even when they/we are unfaithful. Though never mentioned, He remained committed to their salvation. His providential hand is to be seen on the written page. And yes, His providential hand can be viewed on every page of our lives. God, not man, saved Esther and her people.

The Glory Of *The* King

In the book of Esther, we see the fallenness of a human king and the glory of *the* King. Unlike Ahasuerus, our King is a righteous and just King. *The* King of kings doesn't have to be manipulated with invitations to feasts nor does He need to be persuaded to act mercifully towards those who belong to Him. Rather, He graciously invites us to *His* feast! Our King does what is right because righteous is what He is! How wonderful it is for us to know that *the* King cannot act in conflict with His righteous ways! In Christ, we are invited to come before the throne of *the* King. Unlike Esther, we are not left to fret and wonder if we have found favor with our King!

What a radical shift we see in Esther as God turned the heart of the king to bring about the salvation of His people. What a radical shift we see at the cross as the innocent One was made guilty so that we, the guilty, were set free (Luke 23:6-25). He who knew no sin secured our eternal life by paying the full penalty for our sin (2 Corinthians 5:21). Justice was served upon Jesus and now no wrath remains for those who repent of their sin and accept Him as their Lord and Savior (John 3:36). Sons and daughters are now invited to come before Him with boldness and confidence wrought by the blood of Christ (Hebrews 4:16). How favored are we as we approach *the* King? Nothing can separate us from the love of our King (Rom 8:38-39). *The* King's favor will not change like the shifting rule we see in Ahasuerus. God's love for us is steadfast and unconditional!

Consider that glorious moment when Esther finally identified herself with her people so that the king would spare them. Greater still was that glorious moment when Jesus willingly identified himself with sinners. The Father did not spare Him so that we might be spared. Esther risked the condemnation of her king by identifying herself with the Jews, resulting in the condemnation of her enemy. However, Jesus stood condemned in our place and now we are those of whom Paul said, *There is therefore now no condemnation for those who are in Christ Jesus (Rom 8:1)*. Where Esther pled for her people, Jesus now intercedes for all those who are His. Behold the glory of our King!

The King's Justice

I was a hardened criminal by age five. That's right, a pyromaniac before reaching the first grade. My lust for lighting things on fire had been harmless until it escalated one balmy afternoon. My best friend and I found ourselves bored one day in the woods that separated our two homes. Practically living in those woods, we played with our Matchbox cars, tortured small bugs, and built amazing houses high in the trees (or so we imagined). Being the older one, I schemed to relieve us of our strain of boredom. I would slither into my house and sneak out with matches. My friend waited outside while boy genius went to gather the needed matchbook. It was innocent enough; we never imagined causing any fear or harm. We only desired to have a little cozy campfire. Sticks and leaves were gathered as we prepared our camp site. While taking turns trying to strike a match, the unthinkable happened: a match actually lit! To this day, I don't know that either of us actually thought we could strike a match. Shocked and proud of myself, I didn't know what to do. I threw it on our pile of dry leaves and just that fast, we had fire! Being five years old and quite ignorant of how fire works, my friend and I panicked. "Quick," we yelled, "cover it!" Naturally, we began to throw everything our little hands could reach onto the fire. To our surprise, no amount of additional leaves and sticks were able to extinguish the growing flames. As it grew, we panicked! "Run!" we yelled as we sprinted towards our respective homes. Separated, we had no means to get our alibis straight. Before we knew it, the fire department had been called and the screaming of sirens could be heard in the distance. It was amazing how something as exciting as sirens and fire trucks turned into something of incredible dread. The firemen saved the neighborhood by dousing the out-of-control campfire. I can still see the spot of concrete where I stood in the driveway as the fire chief, intimidating in his full firefighter attire, appropriately warned me of the dangers of playing with fire. I remember being more terrified of this imposing figure than I was of the fire! I was sure I was headed for the slammer. I was the one who instigated the plan and came up with the matches. I was the one who actually struck the match. Guilty! To my utter amazement, not only did I remain un-handcuffed (something I thought both policemen and firemen did) but the trucks also drove off after my lecture and I remained in the comforts of my home! How was it that the guilty remained free?

Haman was served justice for his wicked plans. But Esther, Mordecai, and we are not innocent bystanders in the story. If God is a holy God, then how can He remain just by allowing rebellious people to go unpunished?

But now the righteousness of God has been manifested apart from the law, although the Law and the Prophets bear witness to it— the righteousness of God through faith in Jesus Christ for all who believe. For there is no distinction: for all have sinned and fall short of the glory of God, and are justified by his grace as a gift, through the redemption that is in Christ Jesus, whom God put forward as a propitiation by his blood, to be received by faith. This was to show God's righteousness, because in his divine forbearance he had passed over former sins. It was to show his righteousness at the present time, so that he might be just and the justifier of the one who has faith in Jesus.

Romans 3:21-26

We are all lawbreakers of God's holy decree. In Romans 3 Paul is helping us to see that we are not justified by our ability to keep the Law. No, we are made righteous (or justified) by trusting that Christ earned our forgiveness with His blood. Christ's blood propitiated God's righteous anger towards our sin so that His holiness was not compromised in forgiving us.[73] This sacrifice took place to demonstrate His righteousness, holiness, and justice. It was at the cross of Christ where God's justice and mercy met. Full payment was made by Christ's shed blood; this is the justice of *the* King.

The king of Susa was also guilty. Though Haman manipulated the decree of death to the Jews, it was still the king's decree. The ring that sealed their fate was none other than the king's ring. Wouldn't we be shocked if we were reading along in Esther and we came to these words, *"and king Ahasuerus commanded his own death on the gallows, thus ending the edict and sparing the lives of the people including wicked Haman...."*

Astonishingly, that is exactly what the King of kings did for us! Praise be to *the* King who announced the guilty sentence, not on wicked sinners like you and me but upon Himself! Behold our God, *the* King, who died in our place!

---

[73] Learn more about propitiation by reading this brief article by Steve Page: http://timmerwin.com/2017/04/the-big-little-used-word/

Reader, please consider this good news Christ has made available to sinners. God has provided a way out of our ultimate judgment: His Son! We have the opportunity to acknowledge our sin and our need for the Savior. I invite you to repent of your sins and accept Christ as your Lord and Savior so that this gift of salvation would become yours. Please feel to contact me and let me know if you have repented and believed in Christ today. (See contact info at the front of this book.) I would love to hear from you and hear about your story of faith in Christ!

Grace In The Gallows

Even in the death of Haman, we find grace in the gallows. Unexpectedly, the gallows that were constructed to bring death to Mordecai, became a source of grace for the Jews. In a moment of retributive justice, Haman died and Mordecai lived. Haman was dishonored and Mordecai finally received the promotion. Christian, do not grow forgetful of this glorious good news. If you are in Christ, you have been found innocent! Yes, sin remains but we are justified before the Holy Judge. The justice we find in Susa is yet another opportunity for us to worship our God. What grace we find in those gallows! Haman's death brought the Jews life and Christ's death brought us life. Haman was raised on the gallows and the people were freed from the decree of the king and Christ was lifted up on the cross and His people were freed from the wages of sin. Christ atoned for our sin! As we wait for that day when our final promotion will be made complete, behold the grace of our God in the gallows!

Reflections:

- Have you received justice or mercy? Spend some time today thanking God for His unfailing mercy.

- If you are an unbeliever who has yet to come to saving faith in Christ then ask yourself: what keeps you from surrendering your life to Him today?

Chapter 12: **Reversal!**

"It ain't over till it's over"
Yogi Berra

The battle station was heavily shielded with a far superior firepower. It was built to defend against large scale assaults. Yet, it had a weakness!

General Dodonna: *...the Empire doesn't consider a small one-man fighter to be any threat, or they'd have a tighter defense. An analysis of the plans provided by Princess Leia has demonstrated a weakness in the battle station. But the approach will not be easy. You are required to maneuver straight down this trench and skim the surface to this point. The target area is only two meters wide. It's a small thermal exhaust port, right below the main port. The shaft leads directly to the reactor system. A precise hit will start a chain reaction which should destroy the station. Only a precise hit will set off a chain reaction. The shaft is ray-shielded, so you'll have to use proton torpedoes.*

Wedge Antilles (Red 2): *That's impossible! Even for a computer.*

Luke: *It's not impossible. I used to bullseye womp rats in my T-16 back home, they're not much bigger than two meters.*[74]

Every good movie or book includes an engaging introduction, compelling action, ongoing conflict, and a rising hero. The story is built to bring us to a suspenseful climax. It is here that the story shifts, reversing from the initial problem. The Prince slides the slipper onto Cinderella's foot and it is a perfect fit! Luke does the

---

[74] George Lucas, Star Wars

133

seemingly impossible by firing a perfect bullseye into the thermal exhaust port of the Death Star. Against all odds, Frodo carried the ring and saved Middle Earth. Whatever the genre, the problem has been reversed and the characters live happily ever after. Except, while *Cinderella, Star Wars,* and *The Lord of the Rings* are fairy tales, Esther was not.

I am not sure how to convey the full glory of that moment of reversal. Hitler completely reversing his course and sparing the Jews is a fair comparison. Imagine the celebration that would have spilled into the streets as families are reunited! Reversals are a key component to the Esther story. While there was a king in Susa, God ruled from His throne. Because God is God, Haman fell and the Jews were spared.

On that day King Ahasuerus gave to Queen Esther the house of Haman, the enemy of the Jews. And Mordecai came before the king, for Esther had told what he was to her. **And the king took off his signet ring, which he had taken from Haman, and gave it to Mordecai. And Esther set Mordecai over the house of Haman.**

Esther 8:1-2

Reversal, To What End?

A radical turn of events had taken place in Susa! A few days prior, Esther had refused to appear before the king. She eventually determined to proceed, though she feared for her life. Furthermore, though Mordecai's enemy had been defeated, the Jews were still under a decree of death. Oh, the glory of God in the story of reversal! Do you remember how the story began? Mordecai and Esther remained in the comforts of Susa while conforming to the empire. We then found Esther to be a reluctant mediator before the king. On the one hand, God had rescued them and they could have lived out their days in luxury! They had been given the keys to the kingdom. On the other hand, Esther and Mordecai were not saved to then live out their days in ease while their fellow Jews awaited certain death. In a similar way, the Gospel call beckons us to live uncomfortable

Christian lives as we seek to lovingly proclaim the Gospel and rescue those who are lost and dying in our Susa.

Our reversal, not unlike Mordecai and Esther's salvation, was not the end all! Too often and too easily, we settle into the comforts of our redemption. Presuming on the grace of God, we might reason, *"I am saved and justified by the blood of Christ. I am good to go. All is happy in the kingdom of God. I have been given favor from the King. I can now enjoy a life of ease as I live out my days in Susa."*

But we must ask: Is that all the cross of Christ seeks to accomplish? Has Christ suffered that you and I might now live out our days in a life of ease? While our lives are saved as were Esther and Mordecai's, others are still under a decree of death. Imagine if the book ended with Mordecai and Esther enjoying the pleasures of the kingdom, opulence surrounded them while their brothers and sisters were soon to be crushed. We would be aghast! *How dare they live in such selfish luxury! How could they let their fellow Jews suffer and die?* This self-indulgence would have been a tragic and bitter ending. God saved Mordecai and Esther not to further their selfishness, but to position them to then save others. It is distressful when we settle into the comforts that our salvation provides as we live out our days in the Kingdom of God! I submit to you that when Christ said in John 10 that He came to give us an abundant life, He was not saying that He died that we might live selfishly comfortable in our Susa. On the contrary, Christ has powerfully saved us that we might also lay down our lives by bringing the saving message of the Gospel to those who remain under the decree of death!

Go therefore and make disciples of all nations, baptizing them in the name of the Father and of the Son and of the Holy Spirit, teaching them to observe all that I have commanded you. And behold, I am with you always, to the end of the age."

Matthew 28:19-20

I recently had an uncomfortable conversation at my local Starbucks with a stranger. We'll call her Susan. I arrived at Starbucks before it had opened its doors for business. As I walked up to the entrance, I saw Susan looking down at her phone. She too had arrived early. I greeted her with a "good morning." She replied in kind and we struck up a conversation about the weather. "Beautify day, isn't it?" I said. "It's gorgeous," she replied in a conflicted sort of way. While she agreed with my assessment of the day, she did not seem overly convinced of the day's beauty. I noticed she had a bandage around her arm where you might expect blood to have already been drawn that morning. Since we both had nowhere to go, as Starbucks wouldn't be open for another five minutes, I swallowed hard. *Will I live comfortable in my Susa?* This was the question that raced through my mind. At this moment, comfort is what I love! Coffee is brewing just on the other side of those locked doors. I could stare at my phone, check email, and "like" a few posts. Or I could recognize that God saved me and positioned me for moments like these.

I made further small talk and eventually asked about her bandage. That is when the unexpected happened. Susan began to cry! By now, other Starbucks customers had begun to gather and I was aware that they were likely listening in on our conversation. Susan shared with me her recent bout with cancer and her current fight with chemotherapy and radiation. For such a time as this, I uncomfortably pressed forward: *"Susan, I am so sorry. I remember going through cancer. To some degree, I know what you are going through. My body went through more chemotherapy and radiation than I care to remember."* I paused and wondered if I was going to ignore what I believe was the Spirit of God leading me.

Starbucks was set to open in a minute; time was wasting and eternity was approaching. In front of the small crowd, I shared with her how I could never have gone through my bout with cancer if it were not for my hope, faith, and trust in the Lord. *"Susan,"* I said, *"how do you find the hope to press on?"* Tears continued to fall as both Starbucks and her honesty opened regarding her current relationship with the Lord. As we walked inside, I asked her if she would be okay if I prayed with her. And so, in front of a watching crowd, she closed her eyes as I began to pray. As our conversation came to a close, I briefly shared Christ with her and extended an invitation to Trinity.

I wish I could say that she came to faith in Christ right then and there. I have never seen her since. Sometimes I wonder if that conversation had any eternal impact on her. I would also like to tell you that the above story of death to my comfort is a regular episode in my life. But it isn't. Sadly, death to my comfort has come slowly. Unfortunately, I have more stories of the pursuit of my ease than episodes of death to my comfort. God is kind and gracious and I know I am a work in process. The book of Esther helps us to consider why God has brought about this reversal in our lives.

On that day King Ahasuerus gave to Queen Esther the house of Haman, the enemy of the Jews. And Mordecai came before the king, **for Esther had told what he was to her.**

Esther 8:1

I can imagine Esther's stammering as she sought to tell her husband, the reckless king: *"Uhhh, there is something I need to tell you. Something, I should have told you a long time ago.... you know when we got married and you made me the queen.... well uhhh..... I* **am a Jew!** *And so.... Uhhhh Mordecai and I....well uhhh.... we are under your decree to die.....! Sorry, please don't be angry. I should've told you that before!"*

Then Esther spoke again to the king. **She fell at his feet and wept and pleaded with him to avert the evil plan** *of Haman the Agagite and the plot that he had devised against the Jews. When the king held out the golden scepter to Esther, Esther rose and stood before the king. And she said, "If it please the king, and if I have found favor in his sight, and if the thing seems right before the king, and I am pleasing in his eyes, let an order be written to revoke the letters devised by Haman the Agagite, the son of Hammedatha, which he wrote to destroy the Jews who are in all the provinces of the king.*

For how can I bear to see the calamity that is coming to my people? Or how can I bear to see the destruction of my kindred?" Then King Ahasuerus said to Queen Esther and to Mordecai the Jew, "Behold, I have given Esther the house of Haman, and they have hanged him on the gallows, because he intended to lay hands on the Jews. **But you**

137

may write as you please with regard to the Jews, in the name of the king, and seal it with the king's ring, for an edict written in the name of the king and sealed with the king's ring cannot be revoked."

Esther 8:3-8

Have you noticed that playing it safe did not spare Esther and Mordecai? Suppressing who we are in Christ is usually done out of fear as a form of *self-* protection. We need to ask ourselves: how was that working out for them? Believer, have faith in God's redemptive plan. How good is it to know the redemptive storyline of the entire book? God *is* going to have a people, then and now! Therefore, we can know for certain that there are people living in our cities that belong to God.

Reversals Come Because God Is King In Susa

Ultimately, we must come to see that the reason there are reversals in Susa is because Ahasuerus is not the only king on the scene. The Esther story can be viewed as a shortened summary of the Old Testament. I read it and am reminded of Joseph and how many times his life was spared. Conversely, he rose to a position of influence and power so that God might restore His people. Against all odds, Daniel survived because God shut the mouths of the lions. Gideon and his measly army of 300 were somehow victorious. Scrawny David with his sling shot did not defeat Goliath because he was so practiced and prepared. Each of these episodes point us away from human strength and wisdom to the God of all strength and wisdom who brings about the reversal. We must not read the Bible with a man-centric lens. If we did, then we might reply, "praise be to Esther and Mordecai, and Joseph, Gideon, and all the rest." However, when we rightly see the reversal came because God was the King in Susa, we are then in the right frame to behold *the* King who was working out their salvation.

The king's decree couldn't be revoked so yet another edict was proclaimed throughout the kingdom.

And an edict was written, according to all that Mordecai commanded concerning the Jews, to the satraps and the governors and the officials of the provinces from India to Ethiopia, 127 provinces, to each province in its own script and to each people in its own language, and also to the Jews in their script and their language. And he wrote in the name of King Ahasuerus and sealed it with the king's signet ring. Then he sent the letters by mounted couriers riding on swift horses that were used in the king's service, bred from the royal stud, saying that the king allowed the Jews who were in every city to gather and defend their lives, to destroy, to kill, and to annihilate any armed force of any people or province that might attack them, children and women included, and to plunder their goods, on one day throughout all the provinces of King Ahasuerus, on the thirteenth day of the twelfth month, which is the month of Adar. A copy of what was written was to be issued as a decree in every province, being publicly displayed to all peoples, and the Jews were to be ready on that day to take vengeance on their enemies. So the couriers, mounted on their swift horses that were used in the king's service, rode out hurriedly, urged by the king's command. And the decree was issued in Susa the citadel.

Esther 8:9-14

Let us pause and reflect on the flakiness of this king! Can you imagine living in his kingdom? What edict will come next from the decree-happy king? He decreed for Queen Vashti to appear and then declared her banished; he issued a decree of death and then, finally, a decree of life. Ahasuerus was an unpredictable and unstable king. I have found that I too make unpredictable and unstable decrees. I have thought, *Tim, would you please think before you launch into the next decree in the middle of the family room!* While the king's first decree was flippant, it was nonetheless sealed. Consequently, he handed the signet ring over to Mordecai allowing him to create a provision for the Jews. Imagine living in a kingdom that seemingly shifts like the wind. Unquestionably, we *do* live in a kingdom that shifts like the wind!

As the king tossed his ring to the new guy, it leaves us wondering: will it shift again tomorrow? Will Mordecai do something to anger the king? Will Esther be banished at some point, like her predecessor? Living in kingdoms of this world, we never know for certain. And here is why I love the fickle king, his lack of wisdom, and his random decrees. King Jesus is not a random, distant King! His edicts are not arbitrary and we never need to wonder if He will be tossing out decrees in a fit of rage.

While we do not live under a Monarchy in America, we know the fickleness of man's governments. Our study in Esther ought to embolden our convictions. Living in our Susa, we can know our God is King over all kings, presidents, and governments. When the Supreme Court in America makes a tide-shifting decision about marriage, it affects us all. Yes, there are profound implications that come as a result of their decisions. However, the Christian does not fall into despair and fear. The little book of Esther tells us why. The Supreme Court's rulings take place under the rule of a Higher Supreme, the Supremacy of God! The reversals we see there in Susa are grand but they pale in comparison to the greatest reversal in all of history.

Christ died on Calvary's hill and the enemy, Satan, was defeated. Christ reversed the curse found in the garden of Eden in Genesis 3. Jesus did not dismiss the decree of death, He defeated it! Behold your God, *the* King, who kept His decree and executed the decree upon Himself. Praise Him for the glorious reversal of the cross and resurrection!

*Then Mordecai went out from the presence of the king in royal robes of blue and white, with a great golden crown and a robe of fine linen and purple, **and the city of Susa shouted and rejoiced. The Jews had light and gladness and joy and honor.** And in every province and in every city, wherever the king's command and his edict reached, there was gladness and joy among the Jews, a feast and a holiday. And many from the peoples of the country declared themselves Jews...*

Esther 8:15-17

140

Reversal Brings Gladness And Joy

The text tells us that not only did the Jews celebrate, but *"...the city of Susa shouted and rejoiced."* What an appropriate celebration given the dark edict that had loomed over their heads! Walk into any jewelry shop and watch as the jeweler carefully pulls the diamond out of its display and lays it on a black cloth. The black backdrop is used to create a contrast to display the glory of the diamond in all of its fullness. Likewise, the good news of the Gospel is set on the dark backdrop of humanity's sinfulness. The grim reality of our sin and separation from our Creator places the glory and splendor of our reversal on display. The better we understand the depths of the bad news of sin, the more we will join in the celebration of the good news or redemption. The joy in Susa was so great that we are told that, *"...many peoples of the country declared themselves Jews...."* Amazingly, this gathering likely included both disguised Jews and pagan people as well. What a shift in Susa as Jews and Gentiles alike joyfully celebrated in the streets over the reversal of the king's decree.

God is God Even When He is Not Named

When God is not named in Susa, whether by the pagan king or by the children of God, he doesn't cease to be King! Esther then, in part, is about what we believe. Do we have faith that there is a King in Susa? Knowing that God is at work even when we don't see His activity is a source of encouragement, faith, and hope in the days we are living. How are we to think as we live in a country where God is not named? Does God remaining unmentioned limit Him? As our media, government, schools, and culture try with all their might to dismiss God, He is nonetheless King! How certain are you today that there was a King in Susa and how certain are you that the King still rules and reigns today?

While some believers around the world have a decree looming over them to "deny Christ or die," the King is still sovereign. Most of those reading this book will not be faced with the live or die prospect. For this reason, let me bring this home to where most of us live. Is God still sovereign if you and I lose our tax benefits when we give to a church or ministry? Christian, will you still give to the advancement of the Gospel? Or is giving something that Christians do only to receive a benefit? Has God's sovereignty somehow been defeated when He is pushed to the periphery of our society? If we are fully convinced that God is sovereign and He is King in our Susa today, then this life is not our best life; our best life is yet to come. Additionally, if that remains true, then we will not bow our knee, in fear of a king, as we await the opportunity to bow before *the* King. Allow me to bring this one step closer to home. I have often thought that I could and I would take a bullet for Christ. I will not renounce my King! And yet, I am amazed at how easily I cower to mention Christ in the coffee shop. Take a bullet, yes. Suffer a minor discomfort? Sadly, too often: no.

More Reversals Are Yet To Come!

A day is soon coming when we will live in eternal gladness and joy under the reign of King Jesus. On that day there will be a new heaven and a new earth. Esther begged and pleaded to find favor before her king. While that pleading was appropriate before the arbitrary king, no begging is needed before *the* King of all kings. Our King is not a reluctant Savior. Salvation is not ours due to any amount pleading; salvation is ours because it pleases the King to save!

Praise be to God, the death sentence was mercifully lifted and the lives of the Jews were spared. The mediator, Esther, was successful! Praise be to God, the Mediator, Jesus, was successful! There was a king in Susa, his name was Ahasuerus and there *is* a King in our Susa. His name is Jesus and He is reigning today and forevermore!

Reflections:

- How certain are you that there was a King in Susa and how certain are you that the King still rules and reigns today?

- Spend a few moments considering the reversals throughout the Bible and the reversals that God has brought to you during your lifetime.

Chapter 13: Mordecai's War

"What a pity that Bilbo did not stab that vile creature, when he had a chance!
Pity? It was Pity that stayed his hand. Pity, and Mercy: not to strike without need. And he has been well rewarded, Frodo. Be sure that he took so little hurt from the evil, and escaped in the end, because he began his ownership of the Ring so. With Pity."

J.R.R. Tolkien, The Fellowship of the Ring

*Now in the twelfth month, which is the month of Adar, on the thirteenth day of the same, when the king's command and edict were about to be carried out, on the very day when the enemies of the Jews hoped to gain the mastery over them, **the reverse occurred: the Jews gained mastery over those who hated them.***

Esther 9:1

We now come to a difficult section in the book of Esther. There are a variety approaches to troublesome Scriptures. Some pretend that the difficult passages don't exist. Others who feel uncomfortable with a text provide overly simple solutions and subsequently water down the clear teaching of Scripture. This person feels the need to make God's Word more palatable to our modern minds. The last approach is to seek to understand the text as God intended. Since He is *the* Author, we must press in and ask ourselves: *do we truly believe that "All Scripture is breathed out by God...?" What if the difficult texts are provided for us by God, to further reveal God?* If so, then changing the text to make it more palatable or ignoring the text altogether misses the glory of beholding our God.

143

Asking Questions

We begin by asking questions of the text. The obvious question before us is: What are we to think of Mordecai issuing an edict that will bring about the death of others (including women and children)? The subtitle of this book states that God is there, He is the One who is reigning in Susa. Are we to think that *the* King is sovereignly ruling over this part of the book of Esther as well? Or have things unexpectedly spun out of control? It might be easiest for us to simply say *"yes, this is outside of God's control."* After all, what kind of all-powerful God allows an edict that will bring death to innocent people? These are valid questions that we now turn to in an effort to behold our God.

Making Sense Of Mordecai's Edict

Mordecai was given Haman's position. Think about the enormity of this reversal. He exchanged his filthy and dull sackcloth for blue and white royal robes. The ashes he once dumped on his head were traded for a crown (8:15)! Esther, once pleading, had now been given a blank check to form yet another decree. However, solving the problem of the Jews impending death wasn't that easy. Persian law stated that decrees sealed by the king's ring were irreversible. Consequently, the king worked out a remedy as he said to Esther and Mordecai,

"But you may write as you please with regard to the Jews, in the name of the king, and seal it with the king's ring, for an edict written in the name of the king and sealed with the king's ring cannot be revoked."

Esther 8:8

This political maneuvering would be laughable if it were not so serious. With little time remaining, a counter edict was written to give the Jews a means of defense against the original decree. Interestingly, Mordecai's counter edict in Esther 9:9-14 parroted Haman's edict found in Esther 3:13. The only difference was Haman's decree was an offensive attack on the Jews, while Mordecai's was a defensive response to being assaulted.

144

*And he wrote in the name of King Ahasuerus and sealed it with the king's signet ring. Then he sent the letters by mounted couriers riding on swift horses that were used in the king's service, bred from the royal stud, saying that the king allowed the Jews who were in every city to gather and **defend their lives, to destroy, to kill, and to annihilate any armed force of any people or province that might attack them, children and women included, and to plunder their goods,** on one day throughout all the provinces...*

Esther 8:9-12

This new decree that allowed the Jews to defend themselves against their enemies was a form of God's protection against those who had postured themselves in opposition to God's people and His covenant promises. Clearly, there were enemies of the Jews who anxiously anticipated executing the first edict. Therefore, the second decree provided an allowance for self-defense and offered the Jews an opportunity to plunder their enemy, a procurement they didn't use to their advantage.[75]

This decree was not a secret. The enemies of the Jews were made aware of the new edict. Bloodshed didn't need to be spilled and the Jews were not to go looking for a fight. Having been sealed with the king's ring, the news was rapidly carried out and declared across the empire. Two decrees now existed in the land. Imagine: one decree announcing death to all the Jews hung in the Citadel and next to it the second decree granted the ability for the Jews to retaliate.

A copy of what was written was to be issued as a decree in every province, being publicly displayed to all peoples, and the Jews were to be ready on that day to take vengeance on their enemies. So the couriers, mounted on their swift horses that were used in the king's service, rode out hurriedly, urged by the king's command. And the decree was issued in Susa the citadel.

Esther 8:13-14

---

[75] See Chapter 9:10,15,16

God's judgments are always just, always right. That is hard for us to hear, as we lust for autonomy and want to believe man is basically good. We long to live under our own judgment and no one else's, including God's. On the one hand, we are comfortable acknowledging God as our Creator. Paradoxically, some assume He has no right to be Judge. Creator, yes but Judge? No!

We enjoy recounting in the children's classroom how God raised Moses to bring about God's deliverance from Egypt. We instruct them about the plagues of frogs and locusts while appropriately glossing over the death of the first-born children. Noah and his ark make for a cute painting on the walls of the nursery whereas the flood was a horrific judgment by our Holy God against sinful man. Jericho, Babylon, Sodom and Gomorrah were all expressions of God's holy judgment towards a rebellious people. We must recognize that these enemies of God were not only opposing the Jews. They stood in contention with God's covenant and His redemption plan for sinners. This tension can be hard for us to grasp.

The edict can serve to expose this faulty view of God's character and ours. We often retain a low view of God and His absolute holiness. Moreover, our struggle reveals a high view of our goodness. We think: *my sin... is not that bad which means we also do not think that God's holiness is that good.* As we hold to a low view of God and a high view of ourselves, we cling to faulty views that will not allow us to be lead to an appropriate understanding of God's holy judgments. Furthermore, we need to dig in here because this error-filled view directly affects aspects of our walk with Christ.

Worship

A lack of worship exposes this low view of one's sinfulness before a holy God. This devaluing of God and elevation of self directly affects one's worship and growth in godliness. The error of our thinking is helped when we look at Luke 7 and the extravagant worship we find there. The woman who anointed Jesus with her expensive perfume had an accurate view of her sinfulness and Christ's glorious righteousness. She was aware of the lavish forgiveness she had been given by the Savior who stood before her. The realization of the gravity of her sin and the depth of Jesus' forgiveness brought her to an exuberant worship of Him. How was it that others nearby had the opposite response? Rather than appropriately participating in the adoration, they questioned the wasteful and extreme display of worship. Why? Because, unaware of their sin, they thought they were the righteous ones. Not only did they think they were above being in the presence of a sinful woman, but they also held to a low view of Christ for His inability to recognize what was so obvious to them. They clenched on to this low view of Christ and the high view of self.

Self-righteousness does not draw one into the worship of God. It is too preoccupied with the worship of self. That holier-than-thou attitude is why they wouldn't allow for "such a woman" to touch them. As they stood in the presence of Jesus, they actually believed they were the holy ones. Thinking highly of themselves, they were unable to see that *the* Holy One stood before them. Having no grasp of their sinfulness before a holy God, they judged Jesus. As they did so, they were actually judging themselves. They disdained Christ because He proclaimed a divine authority, elevating Him above all others. They arrogantly thought they stood above Christ. In judgment of Jesus, they had no concept that they stood under the judgment of Him.

Therefore I tell you, her sins, which are many, are forgiven—for she loved much. But he who is forgiven little, loves little."

Luke 7:47

This passage reflects how a high view of self and a low view of God operates: As it reverses the roles; we become the judge and He becomes the Defendant. Our self-righteous judgment is proclaimed: *I am not that bad and God is not that good.* Because, in the book of Tim, my ways are higher than His ways. This prideful role reversal is the reflex of our independent, rebellious hearts. We think we are the authority; we long to be the judge, we lust to rule and reign because we think we are a better sovereign and a more able King!

147

When we bump up against the judgment in Persia, we must remember our place. While it is appropriate to ask questions of the text, it is inappropriate for us to stand over it in judgment. While we are asking questions, remember, God is perfect in His holiness and wisdom; He is good, He is Sovereign, and we are not!

Judgment And Grace

God is Holy + man is sinful = a recipe for judgment. While we think we are fairly good people, the reality is that we are not! The question is not: why did God bring His judgment of death on people? The question is: why did He spare any of them? Additionally, why have you and I not been judged? Why have we been spared? None of us are innocent people. The glorious truth is that we are all doing better than we deserve. Therefore, a low view of God's holiness and a high view of self will not bring you to ask the right questions. If God is not all that holy and if you and I are basically good people, what is the point of the cross of Christ? If we are basically good and He is slightly more holy than we are then we are led to ask: *"was the cross really necessary?"* The cross proclaims loudly that we are not good, we are not holy. Christ was crucified to receive the judgment our sins deserved! The cross of Christ doesn't tell us that we are essentially good with a few minor flaws; it reveals our sinfulness and God's perfect holiness. Rather than the cross inflating our view of ourselves, the cross lays us low before Him that we might renounce the worship of self and turn to the worship of God!

Some say, *"wow the Old Testament is violent. God seems to be angry."* While they also say, *"God is a God of grace in the New Testament, He seems to have changed and grown, as He is much less angry in the New Testament. I like the God of the New Testament..."* Has God become more civilized in the New Testament? I submit to you that both the Old and New Testaments reveal our God is unchanging as both Testaments report radical accounts of the judgment of God.

Actually, I must take it one step further by telling you that the New Testament is far more violent than anything we see in the Old Testament. Noah, Sodom and Gomorrah, Philistines, Jericho, and

148

Egyptian judgments pale in comparison to what we witness in the New Testament. All judgments are right judgments. Indeed, there are no innocent defendants in the Bible until we come to that hill called Calvary! Do we read Esther aghast at the new edict, while nodding our head in approval as Christ hangs on the cross? Does the former draw our angry speculations while the other our self-righteous agreement? Only in the pages of the New Testament do we see the sinless and innocent One judged. It is only in the judgment found at the cross that we might rightly cry out, "unfair!" The innocent One died on behalf of the guilty; He was not judged for His sins but for ours!

When we hold to a right view of God's holiness and man's sinfulness, we must wrestle with judgment. All death is appropriate. Indeed, it is what the Bible tells us that we have earned for our sin. In the Esther story, God brought judgment to those who attacked His people. Additionally, Christ brought the war to our greatest enemy: Satan, sin, and death itself. The Father lead the battle to the enemy of His redemption plan. But, in an amazing twist of events, He brought the judgment that our sins deserved upon Himself. That is why we cry, "What a Savior!"

Evangelism

A right view of one's sinfulness before a Holy God also becomes our launching pad into a Holy War of sorts: evangelism.[76] If you are a believer in Christ, then He has saved you from eternal judgment and He now sends you to tell others about what we have been given in Christ. This is our war. Christ came bringing this holy war, not to be fought with our weapons of war, but His!

---

[76] See Ian Duigud for further study regarding the holy war we continue to wage in our day. Iain M. Duguid. Esther & Ruth (Reformed Expository Commentary) (Kindle Locations 1444-1450). Kindle Edition.

Put on the whole armor of God, that you may be able to stand against the schemes of the devil. For we do not wrestle against flesh and blood, but against the rulers, against the authorities, against the cosmic powers over this present darkness, against the spiritual forces of evil in the heavenly places.

Ephesians 6:11-12

Iain Duguid explains that we live in a different era of redemptive history when he writes,

> *We live in the era of the outpouring of grace, in which we fight with spiritual weapons to bring the gospel to the nations, defeating God's enemies by seeing them graciously transformed into his friends. Now we fight with the sword of the Spirit, the Word of God, which instead of turning live foes into dead corpses can transform dead sinners into live saints. Now we wrestle in prayer, seeking God's enlivening work in the hearts and souls of our friends and neighbors.* [77]

God's character did not change from the Old Testament to the New Testament. The Israelites fought defensively against their enemy and Jesus fought offensively to destroy our adversary so that we might now be given new life. Furthermore, the edict of the King still remains and there will be a final judgment. However, while Esther's decree of war was temporary, Jesus' victory is permanent. God the Father brought the war upon His Son so that you and I would not have the war brought upon us! This is judgment and this is grace! Behold your God!

The Judgment Yet To Come

...when the king's command and edict were about to be carried out, on the very day when the enemies of the Jews hoped to gain the mastery over them, the reverse occurred: the Jews gained mastery over those who hated them. The Jews gathered in their cities

---

[77] ibid

throughout all the provinces of King Ahasuerus to lay hands on those who sought their harm. And no one could stand against them, for the fear of them had fallen on all peoples. All the officials of the provinces and the satraps and the governors and the royal agents also helped the Jews, for the fear of Mordecai had fallen on them. For Mordecai was great in the king's house, and his fame spread throughout all the provinces, for the man Mordecai grew more and more powerful. The Jews struck all their enemies with the sword, killing and destroying them, ...but they laid no hand on the plunder.

Esther 9:1-17

There were those who were living in Susa who avoided judgment. Likewise, the future judgment is avoidable for us; it does not have to hang over our heads. While the ultimate judgment of humanity's sins has been suspended at this time, nonetheless judgment awaits the sinner who refuses to repent and trust in Him for the forgiveness of sins. Sadly, most continue to ignore *the* King's edict of future judgment.

Ahasuerus was a flippant king. Frankly, he too easily handed over his ring to Mordecai which allowed him to issue this new decree. Our wishy-washy king had once again flipped, but who knows if he was going to turn yet again the next day. The response of the King of kings who made a decree before the beginning of time is anything but flighty. There is a decree for those who are in Christ Jesus. The decree the Lord has spoken over those who repent and trust in Christ is *innocent!* Your innocence was purchased by Jesus; your sins are forgiven and the judgment for your sins has been paid in full!

Appropriately, the Jews in Susa launched into a festival that spilled into the streets. The celebration continues to this day as the redeemed people of God, shout and proclaim their salvation!

Reflections:

- How do you approach difficult Scriptures? Whose judgment matters most: ours or God's?

- In what ways have you held to a low view of God's holiness and a high view of self?

Chapter 14: Once Fasting Now Feasting

"When God is our Holy Father, sovereignty, holiness, omniscience, and immutability do not terrify us; they leave us full of awe and gratitude. Sovereignty is only tyrannical if it is unbounded by goodness; holiness is only terrifying if it is untempered by grace; omniscience is only taunting if it is unaccompanied by mercy; and immutability is only torturous if there is no guarantee of goodwill."

Ravi Zacharias

*Therefore the Jews of the villages, who live in the rural towns, hold the fourteenth day of the month of Adar as a day for **gladness and feasting,** as a holiday, and as a day on which they send gifts of food to one another.*

Esther 9:19

Three times we are told in 9:17-19 that a day had been set aside for gladness and feasting. The threefold repetition by the author indicates that this was one grand party! Have you noticed, the bigger the reversal the greater the celebration that follows? Hollywood has made billions on reversal stories. Sports are built on the anticipation that your player or team will accomplish the impossible turn of events that lead to victory. Unfortunately, Super Bowl 51 was the greatest comeback in NFL history. I was inconsolable as Tom Brady calmly lead his Patriots from a 25 point halftime deficit to an overtime victory. If you are a Patriot fan, you let out no small cheer of joy when the final touchdown was scored in overtime. I know some of you screamed, shouted, and yelled at your inanimate TV screen. And no one thought it was odd that you did so! Why? Reversal![78]

---

[78] My personal favorite is Cinderella Man: James Braddock, Max Baer, and the Greatest Upset in Boxing History by Jeremy Schaap.

The Esther story leads the reader along as it escalates into an epic turn of events complete with a festival that spilled into the streets. Although Esther ends on a celebratory note, it also leaves us suspended and longing for more. The reason for both the joy and the longing has to do with king Ahasuerus.

Celebrating The Immutable King

Joy explodes off the written page because the seemingly impossible was made possible. Indeed, the *"Lord's arm is not too short!"*[79] As the people of God were staring into the eyes of death, the king's decree spared the Jews. Though he was the flip-flopping king, in the end, there was still dancing in the streets! What Jew cared about future uncertainties? Right now, it was time for celebrating! Eventually, the party would fade and, while this was good for the Jews at that moment, it also had to leave them wondering what tomorrow might bring.

This episode reminds us of yet another glorious attribute of God. Our God, who is *the* King in Susa, is immutable. The immutability of God reveals that our God does not change. Yet another reason to behold our God and join in the festivities!

Of old you laid the foundation of the earth,
And the heavens are the work of your hands.
They will perish, but you will remain;
they will all wear out like a garment.
You will change them like a robe, and they will pass away,
but you are the same, and your years have no end.

Psalm 102:25-27

Jesus Christ is the same yesterday and today and forever.
Hebrews 13:8

---

[79] Behold, the LORD's hand is not shortened, that it cannot save, or his ear dull, that it cannot hear... Isaiah 59:1

The immutability of God is a rock that we can anchor ourselves upon. While everything around us is in constant change, his unchangeableness provides us with a great hope! The question throughout the Old Testament is: Indifferent to the circumstances and in spite of Israel's unfaithfulness, will God restore His people, will He keep His covenant? The unchanging God answers the questions with resounding certainty at the cross of Christ. Did you know that if you are a genuine follower of Jesus Christ it is in part due to God's immutability? You were brought to saving faith because way back in Genesis God made a covenant with Abram. As a result of His unchanging nature, we can look into our Bibles and see that their story is our story. The Old Testament is not far removed from us. Worshipfully, we read the Old Testament stories of how God kept His covenant with His unfaithful people and ushered in their salvation which is now our redemption! God is today who God was in their day! Jen Wilken states: "We fervently need God to stay the same--our great hope of salvation lies in his remaining exactly as who he says he is, doing exactly what he has said he would do."[80]

The glory of God's Word is not that it is teaching us how to be good enough to make it into heaven; the Bible is about the utter failures and sinfulness of man and God's determination to redeem fallen man! He alone purchases our salvation by His blood. The unchanging King has ushered in our salvation and no future judgment remains for sinners who have been bought by the blood of Christ.

This is a glory I am certain my finite mind cannot fully grasp! Praise be to God, His faithfulness, mercy, goodness, sovereignty, and much, much more are immutable! Furthermore, His reversal, when God became a man, makes our reversal possible. We would do well to get our eyes off the body of Christ (His church) and onto the head of that body (Jesus Christ). While we are too easily distracted by a thousand lesser things when the church gathers to worship, our immutable God is *why* we gather. Too easily, our souls grow dull and our hearts lose sight of the glorious gospel truths that call us together to glorify Him. Too quickly, our minds shift from the glory of Calvary to the petty offense that took place in the church lobby. Too often, we

---

[80] Jen Wilken, *None Like Him: 10 Ways God Is Different From Us* (Crossway, 2016), 85.

turn from grace to legalism or license. How is it that we so easily gossip or slander another believer? This gathering of the saints is a local expression of the redeemed people of God who have come together *because* our King is immutable. When the local church gathers, our unchanging God meets us.

Praise be to God, He is immutable and we are not! Indeed, He is committed to changing us as He sanctifies and transforms us to be more like Him! Our change began when He breathed new life into what was once dead. Christ "began a good work in you..." and that work continues until He returns for His Church. Therefore, we gather to celebrate His unchanging attributes and celebrate the glorious, death-to-life *change* He began in us.

Furthermore, when we throw up our arms and proclaim, "I *can't change - I* will *never* change" we must recognize the error of our thinking. We are not God, therefore, we change! "The Unchanging One dispels forever the myth of human immutability, changing a heart that was once stone to a heart of flesh, changing desires that once sought only to glorify self to those that seek to glorify him."[81] While God is at work changing us, and while He is unchangeable, there are ways in which our unchanging God relates to those who belong to Him. He will *never* leave us or forsake us (Hebrews 13:5). *Nothing* can ever separate us from His love (Romans 8:35-39). Christ *will return* for His bride (Matthew 24). The immutability of God is an attribute that is easily overlooked. Yet, this attribute becomes the bedrock in which all His other attributes provide us with comfort and certainty. Knowing the immutability of God David sang: *"For God alone my soul waits in silence; from Him comes my salvation. He alone is my rock and salvation, my fortress; **I shall not be greatly shaken."** Psalm 62:1-2*

Let there be Christ-centered, Christ-exalting, Word-saturated preaching, listening, and singing in our local churches. Strike up the band and let's, once again, lift our voices and sing of His grace! Our King never changes!

---

[81] ibid. 88

156

Esther and Mordecai didn't quite *get it*. Abraham lied and Moses struck the rock. David committed adultery and Samson decided to go his own way. Jonah was a reluctant evangelist and the Old Testament list goes on and on. We roll into the New Testament and the disciples are aloof to the Person of Christ and His mission. Peter denies Christ and Thomas doubts Him. Isn't that the point? Christian, why are we sometimes dull? Isn't it because we forget that Christ is the point and we are NOT? When we start to think we are the point, dullness soon follows. I am a fallen pastor who pastors a fallen congregation. This points us to *the* Point! Jesus Christ redeems fallen man! He never fails, He is the faithful King and He is immutable; behold our God!

Read to the end of the Bible and peer into the appropriate celebratory ending. Revelation is a loud book, containing joyful singing as myriads and myriads of the redeemed sing God's praises. Can you hear the worship as you read the end of the story? The celebration of Christ's victory has provided the greatest reversal known to man!

Fasting and Feasting

The fast in Susa subsided, the people had been delivered from death, and it was time to feast! Fasting and feasting are both appropriate when God is at the center of one and the other. I say this because it is possible to have a *show* of fasting or feasting without any regard for God. As the Jews went from death to life, fasting to feasting, there remains no mention of God! We might expect that this will be the time that the Esther story spills forth in the worship of God who has delivered His people. We await to read, "Esther's song." Where is the verse that says, *"....and all the people shouted loudly, worshiping the Lord who had delivered them from their certain death?"* But, in the midst of the celebrations, God remains unnamed, and it does make one wonder. *Who or what are they celebrating in Susa? Do they see the hand of God in their deliverance?*

Strangely, in our churches it is possible for the music to be of professional quality, the sound mixed to perfection, the singing loudly sung, and yet it can be devoid of worship. Have you ever celebrated without celebrating God? I have, too many times to count. The Gospel is sung and the right words are uttered but little to no recognition of God is being made. Be careful and do not play the Pharisee. There is something of that in you and me today. This tendency is yet another reason why we need the community of believers, the local church. We need more and not less of that community. We need our brothers and sisters singing and worshiping *the* King, stirring us to do the same! We need to see it on their faces, that Christ has delivered us! Behold the glory of our King!

Longing For Our Coming King

And Mordecai recorded these things and sent letters to all the Jews who were in all the provinces of King Ahasuerus, both near and far, obliging them to keep the fourteenth day of the month Adar and also the fifteenth day of the same, year by year, as the days on which the Jews got relief from their enemies, and as the month that had been turned for them from sorrow into gladness and from mourning into a holiday; that they should make them days of feasting and gladness...

Esther 9:20-22

Note that the celebration takes place in Susa and among enemies. In other words, this is not Exodus 15 when God's people celebrated on the other side of the Red Sea, where no adversaries remained on their shore. In Esther, the people of God have been delivered yet they still live in the foreign land surrounded by enemies. The Christian today lives under the decree of our King which draws us into continuous celebration. However, that ongoing celebration takes place among an increasingly hostile environment. While celebrating, one could look up and still view the Citadel of Susa with all of its glory and power. Right there in the face of the pagan king and among enemies, they celebrated. So should we! Join a worshiping community this Sunday, celebrate baptisms, join in the worship found at the Lord's supper, and celebrate the immutable King![82]

The goal throughout this book has been to help us behold our God. Gazing into the multifaceted glories of our God creates a hunger for Him and His Word. My hope is that you have found that Susa and the saints of old are not as distant as you might have once thought. Susa and its god and kingdom exist today; their story is our story.

King Ahasuerus imposed tax on the land and on the coastlands of the sea. And all the acts of his power and might, and the full account of the high honor of Mordecai, to which the king advanced him, are they not written in the Book of the Chronicles of the kings of Media and Persia? For Mordecai the Jew was second in rank to King Ahasuerus, and he was great among the Jews and popular with the multitude of his brothers, for he sought the welfare of his people and spoke peace to all his people.

Esther 10:1-3

As the author brings Esther to a close, we might wonder: *why do we have these three verses in Esther 10?* At first glance, it can seem inconsequential. Esther 10 exists to show us that, even in the midst of the celebration, we have not reached our eternal home! The story ends in the same way it began. King Ahasuerus and his kingdom are mentioned yet again. Indeed, while God's name was never uttered in the book, king Ahasuerus was referenced over a hundred times! Thus, Esther ends on a note that signifies to us that this is not where they belong.

There is still a king, small "k", in Susa. Just as the book began, the king is still pursuing his own interests by taxing the land. The reversal came and, yes, Mordecai is now second in command. Yet, Susa was not their home and Ahasuerus was not *the* King. We are to feel that tension as we read the closing three verses. The king is

---

[82] Resources to help you find a Gospel Centered church:
http://churches.thegospelcoalition.org
https://www.9marks.org/church-search/

still doing what human kings do. This closing, therefore, becomes a glorious ending as it leaves us appropriately longing for more.

Yes, Christ has brought about our reversal. Let there be loud celebrations in response to our new life! And yet, we still live in a fallen world and await the return of our King. It is a wonderful privilege to behold our God today, but we longingly await that glorious day of eternal celebrations. Indeed, we already live in the joy of the Gospel reversal each time we participate in the Lord's Supper but the celebrations are not yet in their fullness, as we will one day celebrate with members of every tribe and every tongue for all eternity!

The King In Susa

Luck had nothing to do with Esther being beautiful and Mordecai's overhearing of the plot to kill the king wasn't happenstance. It was not a random chance that the king could not sleep and that he asked for the chronicles to be read. Let us not belittle the hand of God by assigning luck as the instigator of Esther's queenship and her resulting position to petition the king on behalf of her people. Any beauty that Esther possessed was handcrafted by God as He placed her in Susa "for such a time as this" to foil Haman's devious plot.

What is the point of Esther? Even when God is not named His purposes stand. Where is God in the pages of Esther? He is sovereignly at work, intimately involved in every detail. Never mentioned, He is nonetheless the center of the story and still faithfully saving those who do not acknowledge Him! King Ahasuerus' power and splendor are long gone. Where is his gold and where are the remnants of his glory? Man's kingdoms come and go but the Lord remains enthroned forever! While Ahasuerus is mentioned many times, he is forgotten. God was unmentioned and yet, He is the One we seek to remember.

How big is your God? How big is your Gospel? How grand is your reversal? Is God distantly involved in your life? Perhaps you think that He is involved in the lives of "good" or "important" people like Esther but not someone like you. Behold your God! A big view of God shows us that He is involved in the day by day, minute by minute, second by second details of your day! He made you; He has saved you and you are His. Luck has no place in it.

Yes, Ahasuerus was still the king and yes we too live with an increasingly pagan government but God is King in Susa then and now! The book of Esther fills our hearts with hope in the face of what is seemingly hopeless. Jesus is the King who will come again, taking His people home!

The King Will Return

I love living in this world that God has made; I love my life; my problems pale in comparison with many Christians around the world. God's creation still amazes me, even in its fallen state, it is glorious. It is for that reason, I am in no hurry to leave this world. And yet, this fallen world leaves us longing for our King's return. I hate seeing children, born and unborn, die; I detest hearing about people trafficked as objects; I find myself regularly disgusted with news of humans killing fellow humans. Suffering in this world continues on many fronts.

As we continue to live under a pagan government (king) in our Susa, and as we await our King's return, the question then becomes: what do we do as we wait?

Treasure Christ!

We treasure Christ by beholding our God and living for the glory of our King. We do so by celebrating the redemption He has brought to us. Jesus came into this fallen world; He breathed life into what was once dead. Yes, we long for the day when He will return. While we await His second coming, we treasure Christ by celebrating Christ. Seek to live each day glorifying Him and Him alone.

Grow In Christ!

Though we are justified, we are still in the process of being sanctified. Therefore, one way that we can best treasure Christ while we await His return is by growing in Christ. This seeking of

Christlikeness is the life of the believer. Always growing, repenting and changing to become more like Christ for the glory of Christ.

Proclaim Christ!

What we treasure, we proclaim. Treasure has worth. Whatever you treasure, be it sports, crafts or family, you proclaim its value. No one has to tell you to do so because it simply flows from your heart. While we live in our Susa, let us not be listed among those who did not speak of our God. Let us proclaim boldly to this lost and dying world that Jesus is the King.

King Jesus, thank you for this brief life. Thank you for redemption! Help us to live in this world renouncing its false gods while keeping our eyes on that day when we will be with you forever. Give us the strength to live for you each day and seek to behold you each moment, our God and King, Amen!

Thank you for reading this book!

Please take a moment and provide a review of this book on Amazon!

—